STECK-VAUGHN — TEACHER'S EDITION — LEVEL A

MAPS · GLOBES · GRAPHS

AN INTERACTIVE PROGRAM

Contents

About the Program	T2
Scope and Sequence	T4
Suggestions for Use	T6
Unit Lesson Plans	T7

Remainder of Teacher's Edition following Student's Edition

Blackline Masters

Scarecrow and Symbols	T14
Globe	T15
Compass Rose Game Spinner	T16
Map of the United States	T17
Map of the World	T18
Amusement Park Game Board	T19
Sample Standardized Test	T20
Glossary	T23

Cover Activity: *The description of the activity pictured on the cover can be found on page T11, marked with a double arrow.*

ISBN 0-8114-6206-4

Copyright © 1993 Steck-Vaughn Company.
All rights reserved. No part of the material protected by this copyright may be reproduced or utilized in any form or by any means, electronic or mechanical, including photocopying, recording, or by any information storage and retrieval system, without permission in writing from the copyright owner. Requests for permission to make copies of any part of the work should be mailed to: Copyright Permissions, Steck-Vaughn Company, P.O. Box 26015, Austin, TX 78755.
Printed in the United States of America.   1 2 3 4 5 6 7 8 9 0 DP 97 96 95 94 93 92

INTERACTION MAKES A WORLD O

New Steck-Vaughn Maps•Globes•Graphs

Steck-Vaughn Maps•Globes•Graphs uses interaction to teach geography skills to students in grades 1–6. Hands-on exercises allow students to "learn by doing" and relate those new skills to real-life situations.

As they color, complete, and create maps, students develop practical map interpretation skills and the confidence to use them.

Each *Maps•Globes•Graphs* Worktext® incorporates the content of state curriculum guides, current social studies texts, and standardized achievement tests. Up-to-date, in-depth information in a self-contained format makes this six-book series an ideal supplement to basal texts or an excellent independent social studies course.

Interactive learning at its best!

- **Consistent, six-page units!** Regular pattern increases student comfort level and success: two teaching pages, two interactive practice pages, one mixed practice page, one review page.

- **Step-by-step "Map Attack!" and "Graph Attack!" features!** Reinforce decoding skills.

- **Clear, concise maps!** Present new concepts in a straightforward manner without overwhelming students with confusing detail.

- **Numerous full-color maps and illustrations!** Appealing graphics motivate students.

- **Content-area tasks!** Reinforce math, reading, language, and thinking skills, and more!

- **Atlas maps section in each book!** A valuable reference tool with the appropriate degree of detail at each level.

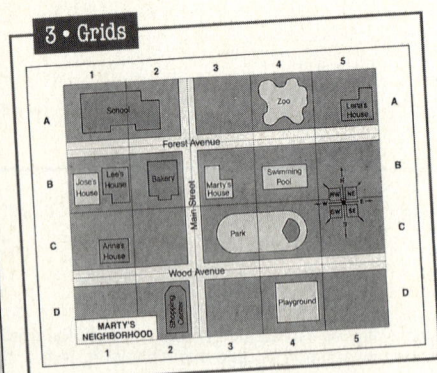

▶ Teaching Pages—Each unit opens with a two-page spread of self-contained student instructional pages. New terms are defined in context, and all concepts are explained as they are used.

DIFFERENCE IN GEOGRAPHY SKILLS!

New Teacher's Editions: effective instruction, minimal preparation

- **Annotated Teacher's Editions packed with features!** Chapter overviews, Scope and Sequence chart, blackline masters, and abundant activities.

- **Lesson objectives!** Identifies clear instructional goals.

- **Vocabulary list!** Highlights new words introduced in lesson.

- **New "Introducing the Skill" section!** Provides a straightforward guide to presenting each new lesson.

- **New "Teaching Notes" section!** Highlights specific student pages that may need extra attention and gives additional activities for using the maps.

- **Extension activities!** Facilitate cooperative learning, critical thinking, reviewing or re-teaching the skill. Link map skills to classroom maps and globes, local and world events, and content-area studies.

- **Blackline masters of sample standardized test questions!** Offer effective practice in test-taking.

- **Blackline master outline maps of the U.S., the continents, and the hemispheres!** Provide additional materials for skill practice.

- **Blackline master of glossary in each Teacher's Edition!** Provides a handy list for student reference.

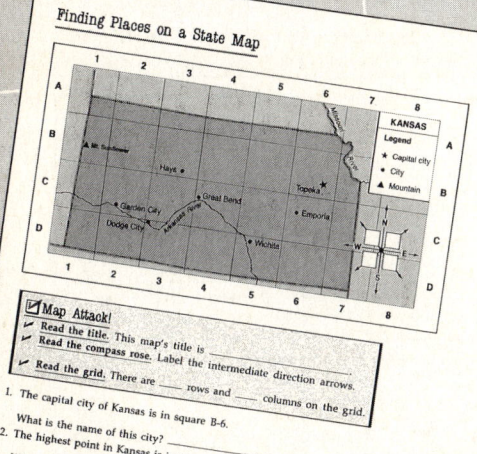

Practice Pages—Two practice pages offer immediate reinforcement of new concepts through hands-on exercises.

Interactive Core—Practice pages provide the essence of the interactive learning experience. Students gain familiarity and ownership as they color, complete, and create their own maps.

Mixed Practice Page—New concepts combined with previously learned skills ensure each student's map and globe literacy.

Review Page—Each review page provides a skill-mastery check and closure on the new vocabulary and content within the unit. Review Pages are also designed as independent work activities.

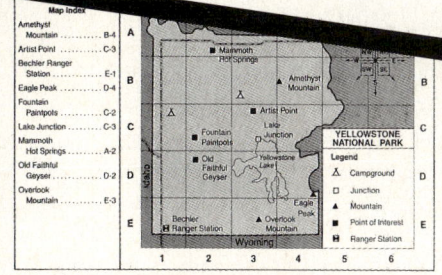

Turn the page for a full-program Scope & Sequence of *Steck-Vaughn Maps•Globes•Graphs*

Scope and Sequence

Numbers refer to the units where each major skill is first taught. These skills are reviewed and reinforced throughout the book and the series.

		LEVEL A	LEVEL B	LEVEL C	LEVEL D	LEVEL E	LEVEL F
Map Recognition	Photo/Picture Distinction	1,2					
	Photo/Map Distinction	3	2		1		
	Map defined	3	2	1	1		2
Map Key/Legend	Symbol defined	6	2	1	1	2	
	Pictorial symbols	6	2				
	Labels	7	7	1	1	2	2
	Legend defined	6	2	1	1	2	2
	Relating legend to map	6	2	1	1	2	2
	Abstract symbols		2,3,6	1,3	1	2	2
	Political boundaries		6	1	1	2	2
Direction	Top, Bottom, Left, Right	4					
	North, South, East, West	5	3	1	1	1	1
	Relative location	4,5,6,7	3,4,5,6	1,2,3,4,5,6	1-8	1-5,7,8,11	2,3,4,5,10
	Compass rose		3	1	1	1	2
	Cardinal directions (term)				1	1	2
	Intermediate directions			1	2	1	2
Scale and Distance	Miles/Kilometers			2	4	3	3
	Use of map scale for distance			2	4	3	3
	Mileage markers				5	4	4
Latitude and Longitude	Equator		4	7	7	8	1,6
	Latitude			7	7	8	6
	Degrees			7,8	7	8	6
	Longitude			8	8	9	6
	Prime Meridian			8	8	9	6
	Estimating Degrees				7	8,9	6
	Parallel					8	6
	Meridian					9	6
	Latitude and Longitude					9	6
The Globe	Globe	7	4	7,8	7,8	1	1
	North Pole/South Pole		4	8	7,8	1,8,9,10	1
	Continents		4,5	7,8	7,8	8,9	1
	Oceans		4,5	7,8	7,8	8,9	1
	Hemisphere			7	7	8,9	1
	Northern/Southern Hemispheres			7	7	8	1
	Eastern/Western Hemispheres			8	8	9	1
	Tropics of Capricorn/Cancer					8	7
	Arctic/Antarctic Circles					8	7
	Sphere					1	1

		LEVEL A	LEVEL B	LEVEL C	LEVEL D	LEVEL E	LEVEL F
Grids	Grid Coordinates			6	3	7	4
	Index			6	3	7	4
Graphs	Pictograph			9			
	Bar Graph			9	9	12	12
	Line Graph			9	9	12	12
	Circle Graph			9	9	12	12
	Time Line			9	9		
	Flow Chart			9	9		
	Tables					12	12
Landforms	Types of Landforms		1	4	6	5	5
	Landform Maps			4			
	Relief Maps				6	5	5
	Physical Maps					5	5
	Elevation					5	5
Types of Maps	Route Maps			5	5	4	4
	Route			5	5	4	4
	Highway types			5	5	4	4
	Mileage markers				5	4	4
	Resource Maps			3	1		9
	Resource			3	1		9
	Special Purpose Maps				1	6	8,9
	Historical Maps					6	
	Climate Maps						7,8
	Land Use Maps						9
	Inset Maps		7			3	3
Time Zones	Time zones defined					11	10
	International Date Line						10
Temperature Zones	Low latitudes					10	7
	Middle latitudes					10	7
	High latitudes					10	7
	Sun/Earth relationship					10	7
Projections	Projections defined						11
	Interrupted						11
	Mercator						11
	Robinson						11
	Polar						1,11

Using Maps•Globes•Graphs

▶ **Maps•Globes•Graphs** is a flexible, interactive program that can be incorporated into your curriculum in many ways. It can be used either as a supplement to basal texts or as an independent course in geography skills.

1. Alternate the Maps•Globes•Graphs units with units in the social studies program. After presenting your first social studies unit, present the first unit of Maps•Globes•Graphs When you return to the regular social studies program, apply any map skills learned to maps that appear in the curriculum. In this way, students reinforce their new skills.

2. Set aside a specific time each week for map study. For example, spend half an hour every Friday on map study. Do as much in the Maps•Globes•Graphs Worktext® as time permits. Related activities, such as map show and tell, could be included in the map study time.

3. Focus on a complete unit of map study and cover the entire program at the beginning of the year, at the end of the year, or whenever best fits your class schedule.

▶ Units 1–7 in Maps•Globes•Graphs progress developmentally. For this reason they should be taught in the order that they are presented in the Worktext®.

▶ The teacher's edition includes a complete lesson plan for each unit (pages T7–T13): student objectives, vocabulary, introductory activities, extension activities, and activities for family involvement. The extension activities involve both cooperative learning and critical thinking and reinforce the program's emphasis on interactive learning. An extensive collection of blackline masters further supplements the activities available for use:

1. **Scarecrow and Symbols** (page T14)
   Globe (page T15)
   Have students color and cut out to practice map skills. Specific ideas for use are provided in the suggested activities for individual units (pages T7–T13).

2. **Compass Rose Game Spinner** (page T16)
   Have students color and cut out to play games described on page T11.

3. **Map of the United States** (page T17)
   Map of the World (page T18)
   Have students use these maps to practice map skills. Specific ideas for map use are provided in the suggested activities for individual units (pages T7–T13).

4. **Amusement Park Game Board** (page T19)
   Have students play this game to practice map skills. Have them color the rides and the squares. Have students move playing pieces around the board, using dice or number cards to determine the number of squares to move. Have students name the direction they are moving at each turn: toward the top, bottom, right, or left.

5. **Sample Standardized Test** (pages T20 and T21); **Standardized Test Questions** (page T22)
   Use this sample standardized test as practice for taking standardized tests. Read the questions on page T22 to students. Have students follow along on their answer sheets and mark their answers to help prepare them for this aspect of standardized testing. Answers appear on page T22.

6. **Glossary** (pages T23 and T24)
   Distribute this glossary to students for reference and review. Have them check each term as they study it in the program.

   Steck-Vaughn Company grants you permission to duplicate enough copies of these blacklines to distribute to your students.

1 • Pictures

STUDENT PAGES 4–9

OBJECTIVES

Students will
▶ compare a photo and a drawing
▶ distinguish a drawing from a photo
▶ match objects in a drawing with objects in a photo

VOCABULARY

photo   drawing

INTRODUCING THE SKILL

▶ Have students look at the cover of the book and discuss whether this is a photo or a drawing. Explain that it is a photo, but the photo includes some drawings. Ask students to identify the items in the photo that are drawings.

▶ Discuss that photos are taken with a camera. Bring in a camera to show the class, and if possible, take a photo of the entire class. Divide the class into small groups. Have several photos and drawings selected to show each group. Have students answer questions orally about details in the photos and drawings. Point out and discuss similarities and differences between the photos and drawings.

▶ Show students a large photo, such as those found on a calendar, of something with a simple shape, such as a hot-air balloon, a piece of fruit, a toy, a car, or a kite. Ask students to make a drawing of the photo and match the colors they see in the photo.

▶ Distribute copies of the scarecrow blackline on page T14 to students. Have students follow your directions about what colors to use to complete the picture.

TEACHING NOTES

Pages 4 and 5 Ask students if they can find things in the photo that are not in the drawing. As students name items, have them underline those items on the photo. Next, ask how the photo and drawings are different. Examples: the drawings are not the same size as the photo; the drawings only show a small part of what is in the photo; and the photo is a picture of a real place that was taken by a person with a camera, but the drawings are pictures of a real place that were made by an artist.

Page 6 Discuss specific items in the drawing and have students circle those items as you name them. Next, have students discuss similarities and differences between this drawing and the photo on page 4.

Page 7 Direct students to draw a red chimney on the roof of the house. Next, ask students to draw a blue car on the street. You may wish to have students add other items to the picture.

Page 8 Initiate a class discussion to have students tell how the school on page 8 is different from their school. You might ask students if their school is made out of brick, whether or not students ride to and from school on school buses, if their school has two stories (or floors), etc. Next, ask students to name things that they see in the photo that are not in the drawing.

Page 9 If students need additional practice comparing a photo to a drawing, have them point out things that are found in the photo but cannot be found in the drawing. Examples: the house is made of bricks, red flowers are near the door, a light is above the door, and a plant is in the center window.

EXTENSION ACTIVITIES

▶ Have students find and cut out photos of various objects in magazines and draw those objects. Then divide the class into small groups. Have students shuffle the photos and drawings and play a game in which they find the matching pairs.

▶ Have students draw or cut out pictures from magazines to create a worksheet that shows absurdities, such as an elephant walking around in a house. On the front of the worksheet, have students write, "What's wrong with this picture?" On the back of the worksheet, have them write the number of absurdities that can be found in the picture they have created. Then ask students to trade worksheets with a partner and identify the absurdities in each other's pictures.

▶ Take a photo of each student in the classroom. Give students their photo, and have them make a drawing of themselves and color it to match the photo. Display the drawings and photos on a bulletin board.

AT HOME ACTIVITY

▶ Ask students to have a family member help them find a photo of something they would like to draw. The photo could be one that someone in the family has taken or one found in a book, magazine, or newspaper. Ask students to make a drawing of the photo and bring both items to share with the class.

2 • Looking Down From Above

STUDENT PAGES 10 – 15

OBJECTIVES

Students will
- compare ground view and aerial view photos
- match an aerial view photo with an aerial view drawing
- locate and match objects in a drawing with objects in a photo

VOCABULARY

photo   drawing

INTRODUCING THE SKILL

▶ Show students aerial view photos or drawings and discuss the difference between ground level and aerial points of view. Have students identify objects in the aerial views. Point out that color is often helpful in recognizing objects.

▶ Have students practice looking at things from different points of view. Give each student an apple. Have them observe the apple from eye-level, from above, and from below. Have students describe what they see. Have them compare and contrast the different perspectives. Then let students eat their apple as a treat.

▶ Take students on a field trip to a high point in the community, such as a scenic overlook, mountain or hill, top of a building, elevated walkway, etc. Have students record their observations, noting what they saw from the high point and what they saw at a lower level.

TEACHING NOTES

Pages 10 and 11 Ask students to circle the swimming pool in both photographs. Ask them why the pool on page 11 looks larger. Lead students to conclude that the pool on page 11 looks larger because the person taking the photo was looking down from above the playground, so more of the pool can be seen. The person taking the photo on page 10 was standing on the ground, so only part of the pool can be seen. Then have students explain how the position of the person taking the photographs affects the size of the tire swing as it is shown on pages 10 and 11.

Page 12 Before students color the drawing, have them draw themselves in the area they would most like to play. Encourage volunteers to share their drawings with the rest of the class.

Page 13 Have students draw a picture of their own bedroom or a picture of what their ideal or "dream" bedroom would look like. Encourage students to label items included in their bedroom.

Page 14 Give students extra practice finding things in a picture by having them count the number of people they can see in the picture (14), the number of street lights (6), and the number of windows that can be seen on the bus (8). Next, direct students to find the woman in the green dress with the yellow hat and draw a circle around her. Finally, have students find the City Bank building and mark an *X* on it.

Page 15 Have students find a simple photo in a magazine and make a drawing of that item, matching the colors in the photo.

EXTENSION ACTIVITIES

▶ Take students outside to the school playground or a nearby playground. Have them name everything they can see at the playground. Make a list of all items mentioned and copy the list onto chart paper or the chalkboard upon returning to the classroom. Direct students to make a drawing of the playground using the items in the list as a reference. Display the drawings on a bulletin board.

▶ Direct students' attention to the cover of the book. Ask them if this photo was taken from ground level or above the ground. Write "ground level" and "above the ground" on the chalkboard to make a chart with two separate categories. Now guide students through the rest of the book. For each page of the book, call on students to tell if the photo or drawing is a ground-level or above-the-ground view. Make one mark per picture under the correct category. Discuss the results.

▶ Divide the class into small groups. Give each group a copy of the blackline on page T14 and three sheets of construction paper. Have students glue the drawings of the car, boat, and airplane at the top of the construction paper, one per sheet. Have them make transportation posters by cutting out and gluing magazine pictures of cars, boats, and airplanes on the appropriate poster. Have the class discuss which pictures on the finished posters are drawings and which ones are photos. Also discuss which point of view is shown in each picture: eye-level, from above, or from below.

AT HOME ACTIVITY

▶ Have students work with a family member to choose an item at home and make two drawings of the item. The first drawing should be looking down from above, and the second drawing should be an eye-level view. Encourage volunteers to share their drawings with the class.

3 • Maps

STUDENT PAGES 16 – 21

OBJECTIVES

Students will
- match shapes and colors on a map with features in a photo
- locate objects on a map
- determine exact location

VOCABULARY

photo   map

INTRODUCING THE SKILL

▶ Have students bring maps from home for a map show-and-tell. Ask students questions such as "What can you recognize on the maps? How are the maps alike? How are they different?" Have students brainstorm a list of different uses for the maps. Display the various maps on a bulletin board.

▶ Provide students with copies of the blackline map of the United States on page T17. Have students color the map so states that touch each other are not the same color.

▶ Have students draw a simple map of the area around the school or around their home. Make copies of the blackline symbols on page T14 for students to cut out and use on their map.

TEACHING NOTES

Pages 16 and 17 Make a list with students of the things that are shown in the photo but not shown on the map. The list may include cars, the railroad crossing symbol on the street, railroad tracks, street lights, water, mailboxes, and various items on lawns. Ask students why they think all those things would not be included on the map. (Accept any reasonable explanations.) Finally, have students circle the house in which they would like to live. Call on volunteers to tell the class why they chose a particular house.

Page 18 Ask students where they think the photographer was when the photo on page 18 was taken (an airplane or helicopter). Next, ask students what the blue rectangle on the photo is (a pool). Ask students to compare and contrast the photo and the drawing.

Page 20 Have students select one pet on the map that they would most like to own. Direct students to circle that animal and write one sentence in the space to the right of the directions to explain why they chose that animal. Make a chart on the chalkboard listing a category for the dog, fish, turtles, orange lizard, and green lizard. Have students come to the chalkboard and make a mark under the name of the animal they chose. Discuss the completed chart with the class.

Page 21 If students need extra practice matching shapes and colors on a map with features in a photo, give clues using colors to describe a certain feature in the photo, and have students circle that feature on the map. Next, describe a certain feature on the map, and have students circle that feature on the photo.

EXTENSION ACTIVITIES

▶ Bring in several aerial view photos similar to the ones used in this unit. Divide the class into small groups, and give each group one of the photos and a large sheet of paper. Direct each group to work cooperatively to create a map of the area shown in the photo. Instruct them to color the map to match the photo. Invite each group to share the map with the class before displaying the photos and maps in the classroom.

▶ Divide the class into cooperative learning groups. Tell students that they are going to make a map of an imaginary town. Have students brainstorm a list of features, such as houses, bridges, schools, stores, fire stations, etc., that they might want to include on their town map. Then provide each group with a large sheet of butcher paper so they can create a section of the town. After the groups have completed their section, tape the pieces of butcher paper together to make a large wall map of the imaginary town.

▶ Divide the class into groups. Tell students they will be making a map of the school, hall, or wing. A tour of the school may be helpful for students when they are deciding what to include. Have students discuss the various areas they will include on their maps, such as the principal's office, nurse's office, cafeteria, library, gym, playground, etc. Provide a piece of butcher paper to each group. Have each group draw a map of part of the school. Be sure each student in the group contributes something to the map. Then have students label each different area or classroom. Hang the completed maps in the hallway for others to enjoy.

AT HOME ACTIVITY

▶ Encourage students to ask a family member to help them make a simple map of their home or a room in their home. Ask them to color their maps, matching the items on the map with the real items in their home. Invite volunteers to share their maps with the rest of the class.

4 • Four Sides

STUDENT PAGES 22 – 27

OBJECTIVES
Students will
▶ identify and locate top, bottom, right, and left
▶ determine exact location using top, bottom, right, and left

VOCABULARY
top   right
bottom   left

INTRODUCING THE SKILL
▶ Have students practice locating top, bottom, right, and left on items in the classroom such as their desks, chairs, the chalkboard, pictures, and books. Have students make labels for top, bottom, right, and left, using construction paper. Have them tape these labels to their desk tops, lockers, etc. Direct students to label their papers for other daily assignments with *top, bottom, right,* and *left*.
▶ Choose items in the classroom and ask students to name something that is at the top of the item, at the bottom of the item, and to its right or left.
▶ Give students a sheet of drawing paper. Have students label their paper with the words *top, bottom, right,* and *left*. Now direct students to draw and color simple shapes in each of the four directions on their paper. For example, "Draw three red hearts at the top of your paper. Draw two green squares at the bottom of your paper. Draw four orange circles on the right side of your paper. Draw one blue diamond on the left side of your paper."

TEACHING NOTES

Pages 22 and 23 Place colored tape on the floor to divide the classroom into sections. Then divide the class into groups according to the section the students' desks are in. Give a large sheet of butcher paper to each group. Have the groups work cooperatively to create a map of their section of the classroom. Be sure each student's desk is drawn on the map. Have students label their desk on the map with their name. After students have completed making a map of their section of the classroom, tape the pieces of butcher paper together to form one large map of the classroom. Then have students label the four sides of the map using pages 22 and 23 as models. Display the map on a wall or in the hallway for others to enjoy.

Page 24 To provide extra practice in finding items at the top, bottom, right, and left of a drawing, ask students to tell on which side they would look to find the tallest building (right). Ask where they would look to find the flag on that building (top), to find the street light (left), and to find the fire hydrant (bottom).

Pages 26 and 27 Make several simple mazes or game boards for students. Make top, bottom, right, and left labels for each game board. Use directions and arrows or simple pictures similar to those on pages 26 and 27. Laminate the game boards or cover them with transparent contact paper so that they can be reused. Allow students to use overhead transparency markers to color the arrows or pictures. The game boards can be wiped clean with a damp paper towel.

EXTENSION ACTIVITIES
▶ Divide the class into groups. Have each group make a kite with the four points labeled *top*, *bottom*, *right*, and *left*. The kites can be made out of very thin dowels or strips of balsa wood covered with paper. Have students make a tail for their kite out of strips of fabric. Have them attach some kite string. Then take the class outside on a windy day to fly the kites.
▶ Play a game of "I Spy" with students, using *top*, *bottom*, *right*, and *left* in your clues. For example, you might say, "I spy with my little eye something that is at the top of the blue bulletin board."
▶ Divide the class into pairs of students. Give each pair a copy of the game board blackline on page T19, a number cube, and two tokens. Have students color their game board and make up a game that practices using top, bottom, left, and right. Allow students time to play the game they have made up so they can evaluate it. Then have each pair of students explain to the class the rules of the game they created.
▶ On the chalkboard or a large sheet of paper, draw a bookshelf with two shelves. Draw simple toys on the shelves, leaving spaces for students to add toys. Ask students to identify which toys are on the top shelf and which toys are on the bottom shelf. Ask which toys are on the right side and which ones are on the left side. Ask volunteers to draw a toy in an empty space. Have students describe its location.

AT HOME ACTIVITY
▶ Have students ask a family member to help them make a list of items in their home that have four sides, such as a refrigerator, bed, TV, etc. Encourage students to share their lists with the class. Make a list on the chalkboard of items mentioned by students.

5 • Four Directions

STUDENT PAGES 28–33

OBJECTIVES

Students will
- locate south, east, and west in relation to north
- determine exact location using direction
- recognize N, S, E, and W as abbreviations for north, south, east, and west

VOCABULARY

north   south   east   west

INTRODUCING THE SKILL

- Take students outside on a sunny day at noon and have them face their shadows. They will be facing north. South will be behind them. East will be to their right, and west will be to their left. Have students locate landmarks in each direction.

▶▶ *This activity is pictured on the cover.* Have copies of the scarecrow on page T14 ready for students to color, cut out, and paste in the center of a large sheet of paper. (To make the scarecrow stand up, mount it on posterboard with tabs added to its feet.) Direct students to label the paper with an *N* at the top, *S* at the bottom, *E* on the right, and *W* on the left. Now have students illustrate the landmarks they saw in each direction during the activity above.

- Determine the four cardinal directions inside the classroom and tape a label in each direction. Have students name items in each direction.

TEACHING NOTES

Page 28 Take students outside to a sidewalk or paved area on the playground. Using a compass and several different colors of chalk, draw the outline for two or three compass roses similar to the one on page 28. Divide the class into groups. Have students color each compass rose with the chalk and label the four cardinal directions with *N*, *S*, *E*, and *W*. Have students take turns standing in the center of their compass rose while you call out a direction. Have the student in each compass rose name an object in that direction.

Page 29 Ask students which direction the farmer is facing (north). Ask students if they can find any other things in the north part of the farm besides the barn (trees and the field). Have students draw a line from the farmer's right hand to the object on the farm that he is pointing to (haystack), and direct them to circle it. Next, have students draw a line from the farmer's left hand to the object he is pointing to (truck), and have them make an *X* on it. Now ask which direction the farmer would be facing if he turned around (south).

Page 30 If students have difficulty with cardinal directions, give them additional practice before progressing to page 31, which introduces the direction of movement.

Page 31 When using this page, remind students that they need to pay close attention to the direction they are moving, regardless of where they start on the map. Read and work through the first item with students. Ask them to place a finger on the word *start* at the flower gardens. Have them move their finger in the direction to get to the ducks. Have them draw an arrow showing this path. Ask students to name and circle the correct letter for the direction they moved. You may wish to work through additional items with students. Then have students identify other things that they would pass as they make a path through the park and tell which direction each thing is from the path.

Page 32 Have students name the directions they would go if they started at the popcorn stand and went in the reverse order to get back to the gate.

Page 33 Using a compass to determine direction, take the class to the school library. Starting at the door, select items such as the globe, card catalog, etc., and have students determine which direction they would go to get from one item to another.

EXTENSION ACTIVITIES

- Provide students with copies of the compass rose blackline on page T16. Have them follow the directions to make the compass rose game spinner. The spinner can be used to play the following games.
  - Students take turns spinning the direction arrow. They identify the direction closest to the arrow and then name something found in that direction in the classroom.
  - Have students use the map on pages 46 and 47 as a game board. They will need small playing pieces or markers. Each player places a marker on the state of Kansas. Students take turns with the game spinner and move their markers to the next state in the direction the spinner indicates. The first student to reach a large body of water wins the game.

AT HOME ACTIVITY

- Have students draw a picture of the outside of their home. Then encourage them to have a family member help them determine which direction their home faces and label the drawing with *N*, *S*, *E*, and *W*.

6 • Symbols and Map Keys

STUDENT PAGES 34–39

OBJECTIVES

Students will

▶ match map key symbols with symbols on a map

▶ add symbols to a map

▶ determine relative location using direction

▶ distinguish a symbol from a photo

VOCABULARY

symbol   map key

INTRODUCING THE SKILL

▶ Have students identify symbols they use at school (+, –, =, $, and ¢ for add, subtract, equals, dollars, and cents). List familiar symbols such as color on traffic lights, various road signs, and holiday symbols like pumpkins, turkeys, and hearts. Now have students make up symbols for common items.

▶ Have students practice identifying symbols on map keys using maps found in the classroom, library, or basal textbooks. Ask for volunteers to find matching symbols on the maps.

▶ Using chart paper or poster board, make a chart or graph that the entire class can fill in with a symbol for their eye or shoe color. Have each student draw and color a pair of eyes or shoes above the label of their own eye or shoe color. Discuss the chart and use of symbols.

TEACHING NOTES

Pages 34 and 35 Explain to students that symbols are often used on maps to stand for something that is real. Discuss how a map key unlocks a map. Have students read the label next to each symbol on the map key on page 35. Then have them draw a line to connect each symbol in the map key to its matching symbol on the map.

Pages 36 and 37 Take students on a walk through the neighborhood surrounding your school. Direct students to find at least three things that they could draw a symbol for. Upon returning to class, have students draw, color, and cut out their symbols. Draw a simple picture or symbol of the school in the center of a large sheet of butcher paper. Create a map of the neighborhood by pasting the students' symbols around the school. Students can then add streets, cars, buses, etc., to the map. Display the map on a bulletin board or in the hallway.

Page 38 Direct students to find the school on the map. Have them draw a line and tell you which direction they would be going from the school to the large house (west). Now have students draw a line and tell which direction they would be going from the large house to the two trees that have not been colored (south). Direct them to color the trees orange. Next, have students draw a line and tell which direction they would be going from the trees to the store (east) and then from the store to the factory (north).

EXTENSION ACTIVITIES

▶ Give students copies of the blackline map of the United States on page T17. Ask students to color one state in each section (north, south, east, west) of the country that they would like to visit. Then have students pretend to take a trip to the states they have colored. Ask them to write a story about their trip.

▶ Have copies of the blackline on page T14 available for students to use. Have students draw maps of their classroom, playground, or neighborhood. Students can draw their own symbols or use the symbols from page T14 to make a map key.

▶ Divide the class into groups. Help each group to design and create a Monopoly-like game board where students can create their own symbols in each of the squares. Some symbols can be for bad luck, where the player is sent backward, and others can be for good luck, where the player is sent ahead or gets an extra turn. Each time players pass start, they earn a symbol card (perhaps a card with a sticker or happy face on it). Reading or math flash cards can be used to play this game. If students read the word or solve the math problem correctly, they get to roll the dice and move on the game board. The player with the most symbol cards at the end of the game wins.

▶ Divide the class into cooperative learning groups. Provide each group with a copy of the blackline map of the world on page T18. Help students do research to find out what interesting animals, plants, or natural features are found on each continent. Have students create symbols to present the information on their map. Be sure they add a map key to the map so their symbols can be understood. Ask each group to explain the information shown on their map.

AT HOME ACTIVITY

▶ Invite students to have a family member help them create symbols for three items in their home.

NOTE: Go to the back of the student book for page T13.

STECK-VAUGHN

MAPS · GLOBES · GRAPHS

AN INTERACTIVE PROGRAM

LEVEL A

Writer
Henry Billings

Consultants

Marian Gregory
Teacher
San Luis Coastal Unified
  School District
San Luis Obispo, California

Norman McRae, Ph.D.
Former Director of Fine
  Arts and Social Studies
Detroit Public Schools
Detroit, Michigan

Marilyn Nebenzahl
Social Studies Consultant
San Francisco, California

Gloria Sesso
Supervisor of Social Studies
Half Hollow Hills School
  District
Dix Hills, New York

Edna Whitfield
Former Social Studies
  Supervisor
St. Louis Public Schools
St. Louis, Missouri

Karen Wiggins
Director of Social Studies
Richardson Independent
  School District
Richardson, Texas

STECK-VAUGHN
COMPANY
A Subsidiary of National Education Corporation

Acknowledgments

Staff Credits Executive Editor: Diane Sharpe
Project Editor: Anne Souby
Art Director: D. Childress
Designer: Richard Balsam

Cover Design Linda Adkins Graphic Design

Cover Photography Cooke Photographics

Photography Rick Williams–4
David McKenzie–8, 9, 22, 28, 40 (globe)
Stan Kearl–10, 11, 15, 34 (sheep, horse, truck)
David Phillips–16, 18
Gary Russ–19
© Mark Segal/TSW-Click/Chicago–21
© Larry Lefever/Grant Heilman Photography–34 (barn)
© Index Stock International Inc.–40 (earth)

Illustration Holly Cooper–4, 7–9, 17–20
David Griffin–5, 6, 21, 31, 32, 39
Michael Krone–12–15, 29–30, 33
T.K. Riddle–23–27, 34–38

Cartography Land Registration and Information Service
    Amherst, Nova Scotia, Canada
Maryland Cartographics Incorporated

ISBN 0-8114-6200-5

Copyright © 1993 Steck-Vaughn Company.
All rights reserved. No part of the material protected by this copyright may be reproduced or utilized in any form or by any means, electronic or mechanical, including photocopying, recording, or by any information storage and retrieval system, without permission in writing from the copyright owner.
Requests for permission to make copies of any part of the work should be mailed to: Copyright Permissions, Steck-Vaughn Company, P.O. Box 26015, Austin, TX 78755.
Printed in the United States of America.

Contents

1 • Pictures 4

2 • Looking Down From Above 10

3 • Maps 16

4 • Four Sides 22

5 • Four Directions 28

6 • Symbols and Map Keys 34

7 • Globes 40

Atlas 46

1 • Pictures

This is a **photo**.
It is a picture made by a  .

SKILL: READING PICTURES

Name _____

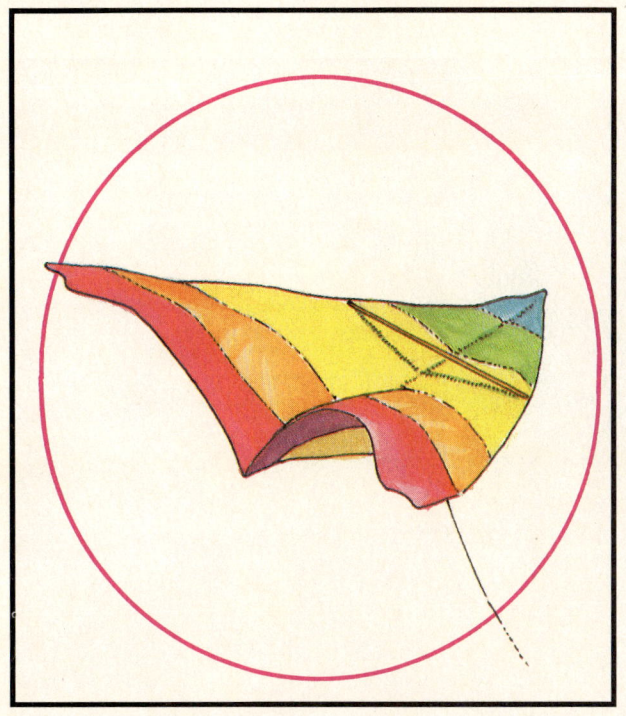

These are **drawings**.
Which drawings are of things in the photo?
Circle them.

READING PICTURES

Finding Things in a Picture

This is a drawing of the photo.
It shows the same place.

1. Color the shirt red. Color the pants blue.
2. Color the dog brown.   **Colored to match the directions**
3. Color the kite.

6 PRACTICE

Name _____

Finding Things in a Picture

This drawing shows a house.

1. Color the doors brown.
2. Color the trees green.
3. Color the steps yellow.

Match a Photo and a Drawing

Color the rest of the drawing. **Colors similar to the photo**
Match the colors you see in the photo.

MIXED PRACTICE

Name _____

Skill Check

Words I Know **photo drawing**

Write each word under a picture.

photo

drawing

Reading a Picture

1. Color the house yellow. **Colored to match the directions**
2. Color the bicycle red.
3. Color the car blue.

REVIEW

2 • Looking Down From Above

This photo shows a park.
It was taken from the ground.
What things do you see?

SKILL: READING AERIAL PHOTOS

Name _____

This photo shows the same park.
It was taken from above.
What else do you see?

Finding Things in a Picture

This drawing shows the same park.

1. Color the trees and grass green.
2. Color the pool blue.
3. Color the swing yellow.
4. Color the fence brown.

Colored to match the directions

Name _____

Finding Things in a Picture

What does this drawing show?

1. Color the bed blue. **Colored to match the directions**
2. Color the table yellow.
3. Color the books green.
4. Color the toys red.

Finding Things in a Picture

What does this drawing show?

1. Color the bus yellow.
2. Color one car red.
3. Color two cars blue.
4. Color the truck orange.

Colored to match the directions

Name _____

Skill Check

Color the drawing of the beach. **Colors similar to the photo**
Match the colors you see in the photo.

REVIEW 15

3 • Maps

This photo shows a neighborhood.
What do you see in the photo?

SKILL: AERIAL PHOTOS AND MAPS

Name _____

Here is the same neighborhood.
This is a **map.**

Colored to match the directions

1. Two houses are not colored. Color them yellow.
2. Find the streets. Color them gray.

AERIAL PHOTOS AND MAPS

Making a Map From a Photo

1. Draw the pool on the map. Color it blue.
2. Color the rest of the map. **Colors similar to the photo**
   Match the colors you see in the photo.

Name _____

Making a Map From a Photo

1. Some cars are missing on the map.
   Add them to the map.
2. Color the rest of the map.   **Colors similar to the photo**
   Match the colors you see in the photo.

PRACTICE **19**

Finding Things on a Map

This map shows a pet store.

1. Color the fish orange.
2. Color the dog brown.
3. Add a turtle to the map.
4. Color the turtles green.

Colored to match the directions

MIXED PRACTICE

Name _____

Skill Check

Words I Know   map

Write the word <u>map</u> under the map.
Write the word <u>photo</u> under the photo.

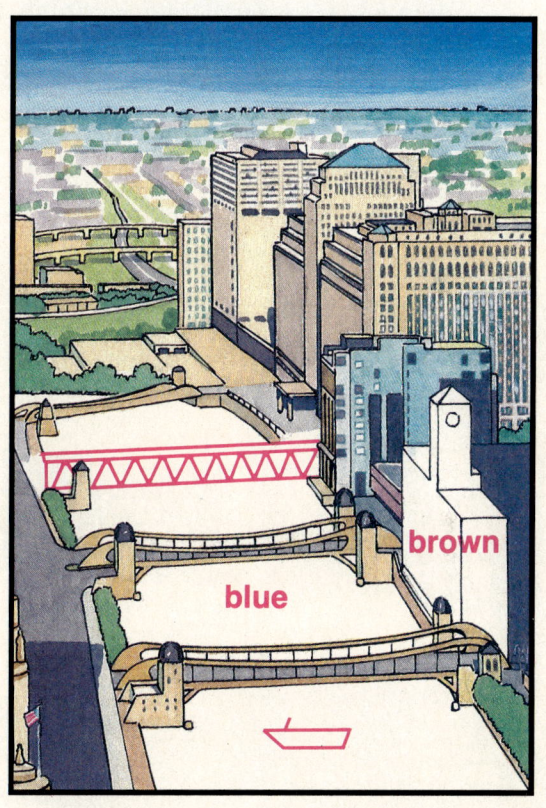

brown
blue

----
photo

----
map

1. Look at the map. Color the building brown.
2. Add the boat to the map.   **Colored and drawn to match the directions**
3. Add the bridge to the map.
4. Color the water blue.

REVIEW **21**

4 • Four Sides

This photo has four sides.

The blackboard is at the **top**.

The desks are at the **bottom**.

The flag is at the **right**.

The globe is at the **left**.

Name _____

This is a map of a classroom.

Colored to match the directions

1. Color the blackboard at the top green.
2. Color the desks at the bottom yellow.
3. Color the flagpole at the right red.
4. Color the globe at the left blue.

Finding Four Sides

1. Write <u>top</u>, <u>bottom</u>, <u>right</u> and <u>left</u> in the boxes.
2. Color the plane at the top red.   **Colored to match the directions**
3. Color the sidewalk at the bottom brown.
4. Color the bus on the right yellow.
5. Color the car on the left green.

Name _____

Finding Four Sides

1. Write <u>top</u>, <u>bottom</u>, <u>right</u> and <u>left</u> in the boxes.
2. Color two lions near the top yellow. **Colored to match the directions**
3. Color three monkeys near the bottom brown.
4. Color one elephant near the right gray.
5. Color four parrots near the left green.

PRACTICE 25

Moving Toward Top, Bottom, Right, or Left

1. Write top, bottom, right and left in the boxes.
2. One arrow points to the top. Color it red.
3. One arrow points to the right. Color it green.
4. One arrow points to the bottom. Color it yellow.
5. One arrow points to the left. Color it blue.
6. Color the carrots.

Name _____

Skill Check

Words I Know   top   bottom   right   left

This map shows a living room.

1. Write <u>top</u>, <u>bottom</u>, <u>right</u> and <u>left</u> in the boxes.
2. Draw a sofa near the top.
3. Draw a TV near the bottom.
4. Color the chair near the right green.
5. Color the chair near the left brown.

REVIEW

5 • Four Directions

North, south, east, and west are directions.
N, S, E, and W stand for north, south, east, and west.

The girl faces **north**. Find N in the photo.
South is behind her. Find S in the photo.
East is to her right. Find E in the photo.
West is to her left. Find W in the photo.

Name _____

This map shows a farm.
The top of the map is north.

Where is each thing?
Write north, south, east, and west.

- barn: north
- haystack: east
- truck: west
- cow: south

DIRECTIONS 29

Finding Directions at the Fruit Market

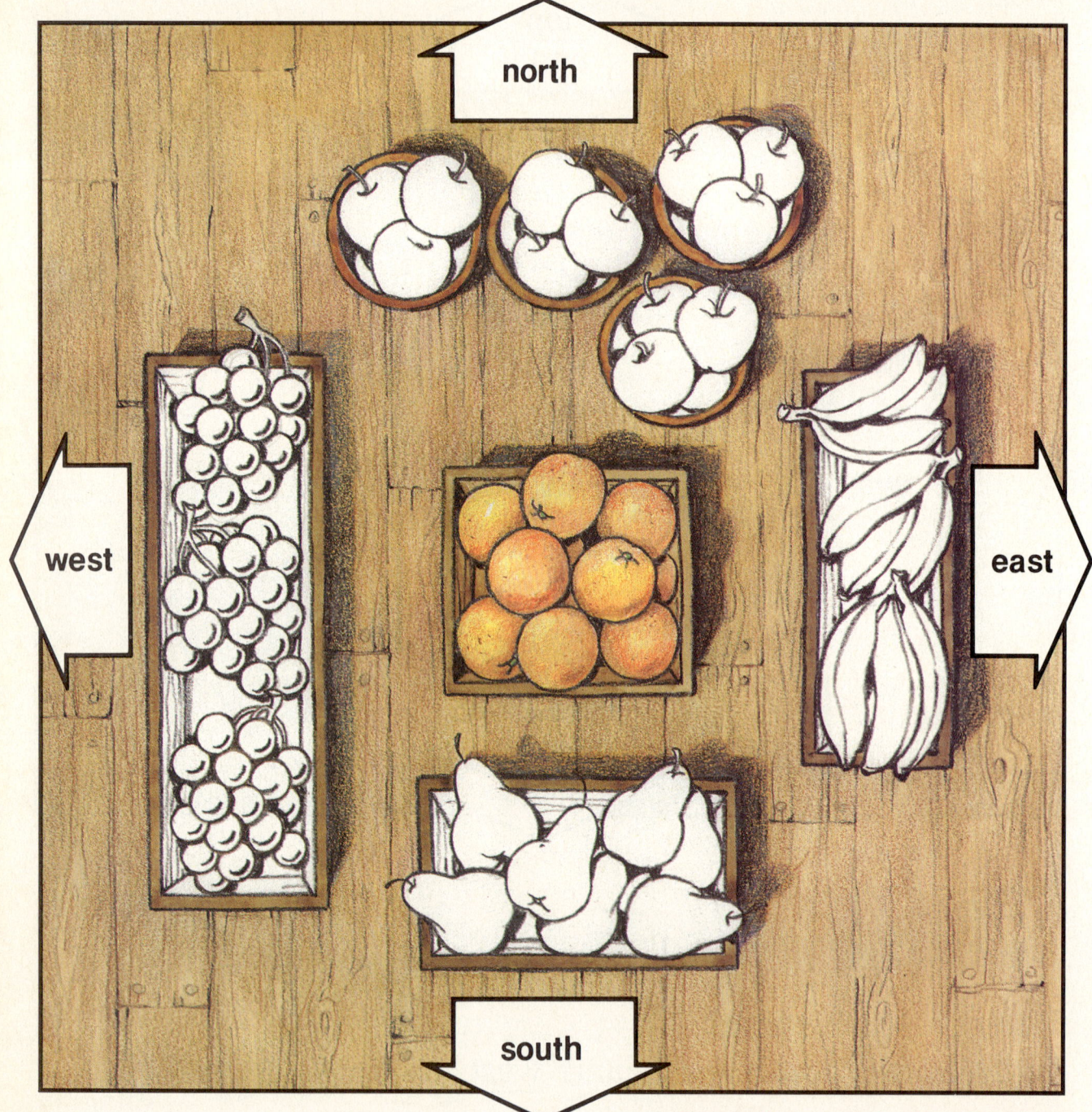

Colored to match the directions

1. Which fruit is on the north side? Color it red. **apples—north**
2. Which fruit is on the south side? Color it green. **pears—south**
3. Which fruit is on the east side? Color it yellow. **bananas—east**
4. Which fruit is on the west side? Color it purple. **grapes—west**

Name _____

Finding Directions at the Park

Start at the flower gardens.
Draw an arrow to show where you go.
Then circle the letter of the direction you go.

1. Go to feed the . You go Ⓝ E.

2. Next go to the . You go S Ⓦ.

3. Then go to the . You go Ⓢ N.

4. Now run to the . You run W Ⓔ.

PRACTICE 31

Finding Directions at the Fair

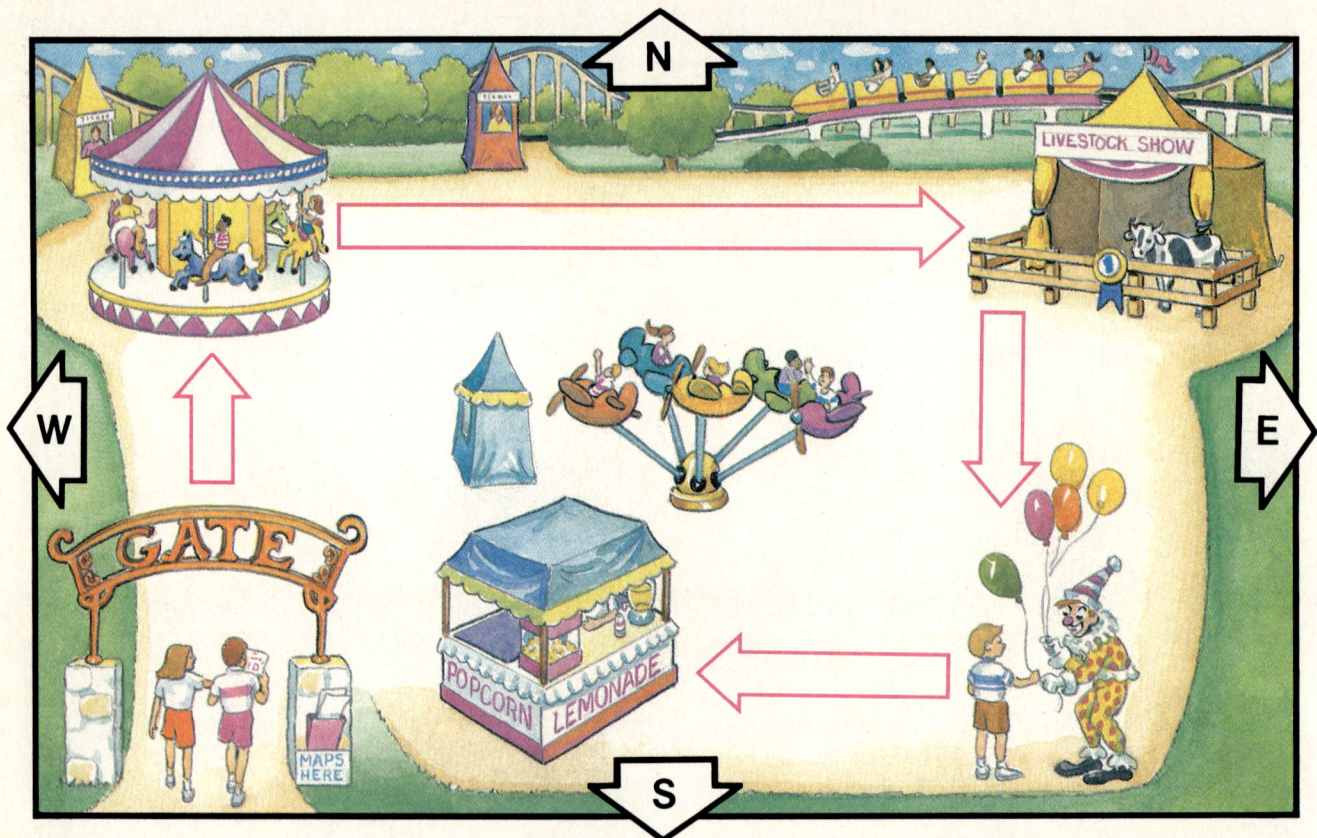

Get a map at the gate and have fun at the fair.
Draw an arrow to show where you go.
Write the direction you go to get

① from 🎪GATE to 🎠 . __N or north__

② from 🎠 to 🐄 . __E or east__

③ from 🐄 to 🤡 . __S or south__

④ from 🤡 to 🍿 . __W or west__

32 MIXED PRACTICE

Name _____

Skill Check

Words I Know   north   south   east   west

Finding Directions on a Map

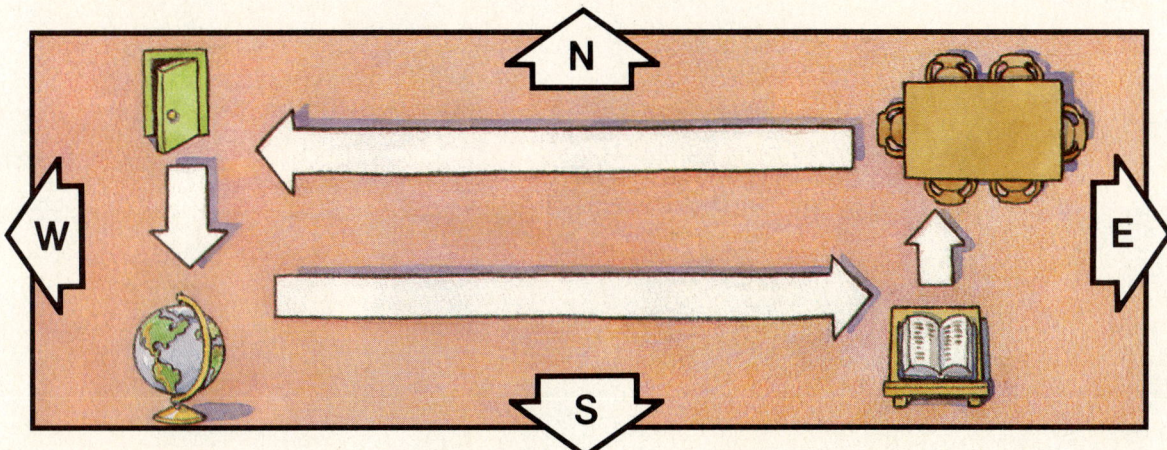

This map shows a library.

Write the direction that tells the way to get

① from  to  . _____ south _____

② from  to  . _____ east _____

③ from  to  . _____ north _____

④ from  to  . _____ west _____

REVIEW 33

6 • Symbols and Map Keys

The photo shows a real barn.
The drawing is a **symbol** for a barn.
A symbol stands for something real.

Match each symbol with a photo.

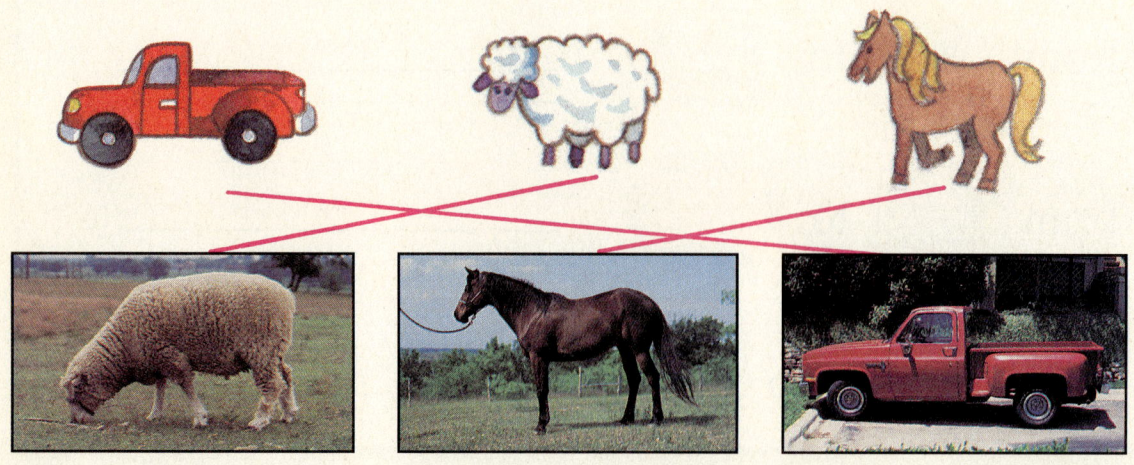

SKILL: SYMBOLS AND MAP KEYS

Name _____

This map shows a farm.
The **map key** tells what each symbol stands for.

Write what the symbols stand for.
The first one is done for you.

house   barn

horse   sheep

SYMBOLS AND MAP KEYS 35

Finding Symbols on a Map

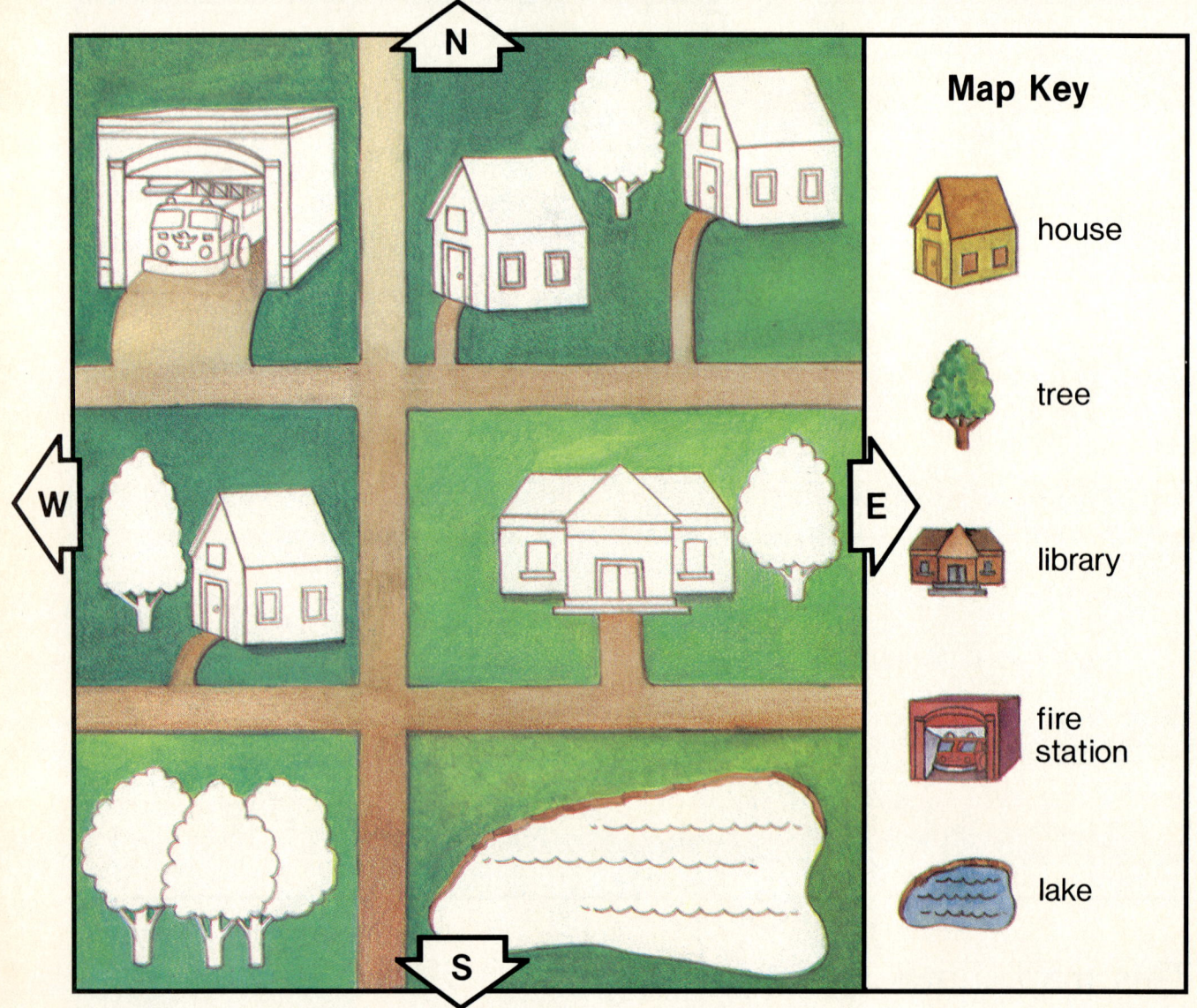

1. Find <u>N</u>, <u>S</u>, <u>E</u>, and <u>W</u> on the map.
2. Study the map key.
3. Find the trees on the map. Color them green.
4. Find the houses. Color them yellow.
5. Find the library. Color it brown.
6. Find the fire station. Color it red.
7. Find the lake. Color it blue.

Colored to match the directions

Name _____

Finding Symbols on a Map

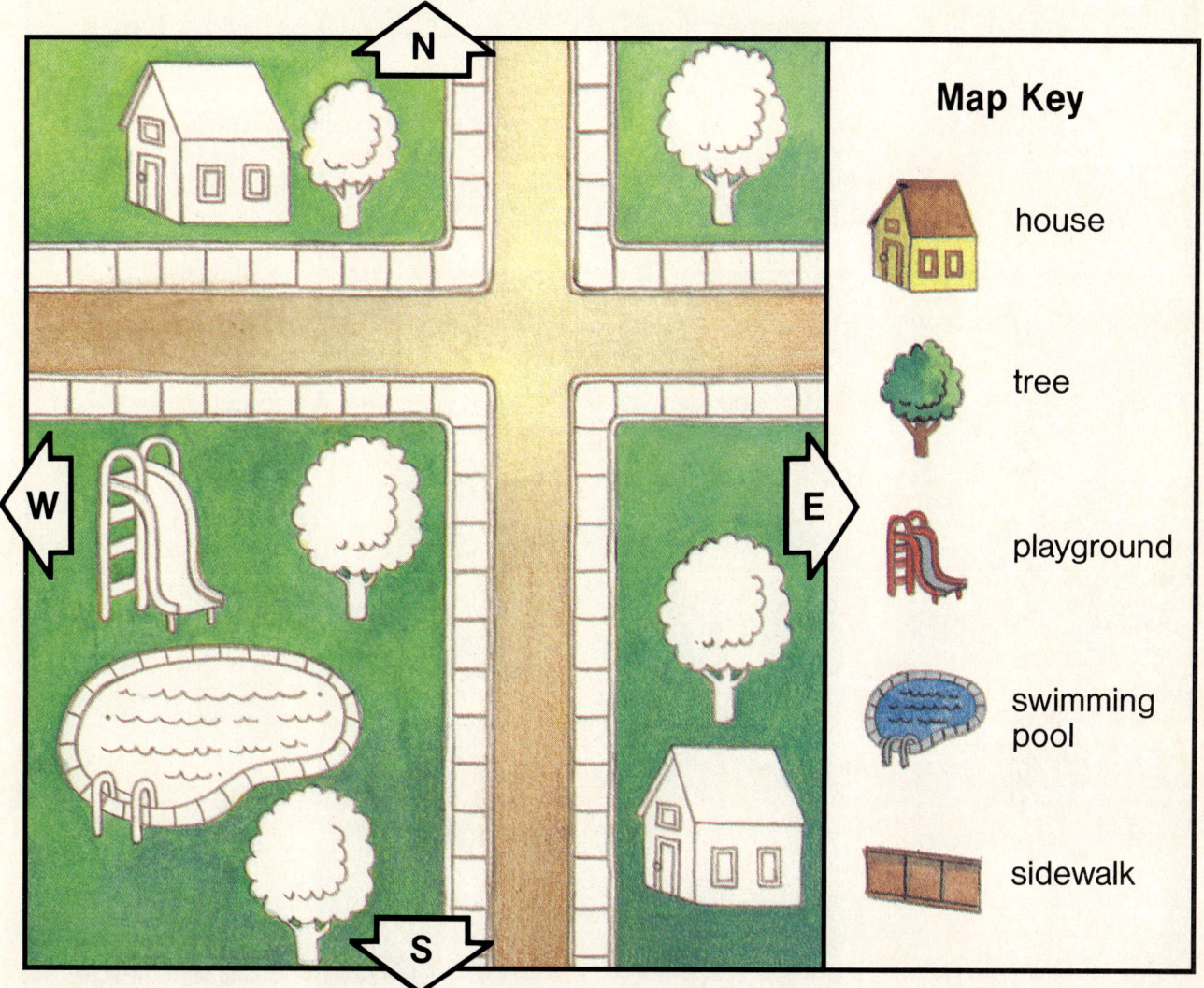

1. Find <u>N</u>, <u>S</u>, <u>E</u>, and <u>W</u> on the map.
2. Study the map key.
3. Find the houses on the map. Color them yellow.
4. Find the trees. Color them green. **Colored to match the directions**
5. Find the playground. Color it red.
6. Find the swimming pool. Color it blue.
7. Find the sidewalks. Color them brown.

Finding Symbols on a Map

1. Write <u>N</u>, <u>S</u>, <u>E</u>, and <u>W</u> where they belong.
2. Find the factory. Go south. Color that tree red.
3. Find the library. Go north. Color that tree blue.
4. Find the store. Go east. Color that tree green.
5. Find the school. Go west. Color that tree yellow.

Name _____

Skill Check

Words I Know   **symbol**   **map key**

_____

The _____**map key**_____ tells what each symbol stands for.

Reading a Map

This map shows a farm.

1. Write <u>N</u>, <u>S</u>, <u>E</u>, and <u>W</u> where they belong.
2. Find the horses. Color them brown.
3. Find the barn. Color it red.
4. Find the house. Go west. Color that tree green.

7 • Globes

The large photo shows the earth.
The earth is round like a ball.

The small photo shows a **globe**.
A globe is also round like a ball.
A globe is a **model** of the earth.

SKILL: GLOBES

Name _____

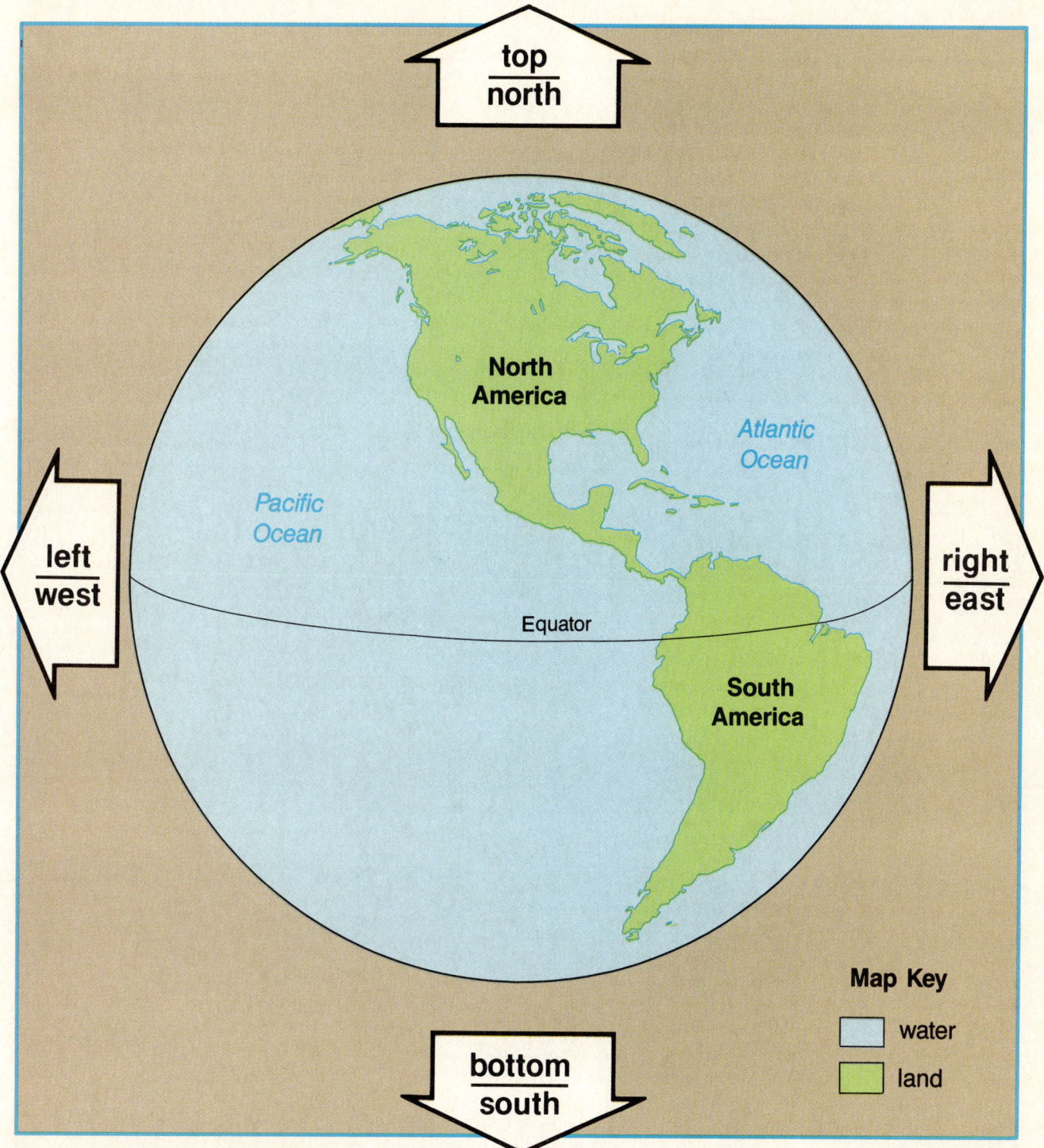

Look at the globe above.
The blue color stands for water.
The green color stands for land.
The words are names of real places.

GLOBES 41

Finding Places on a Globe

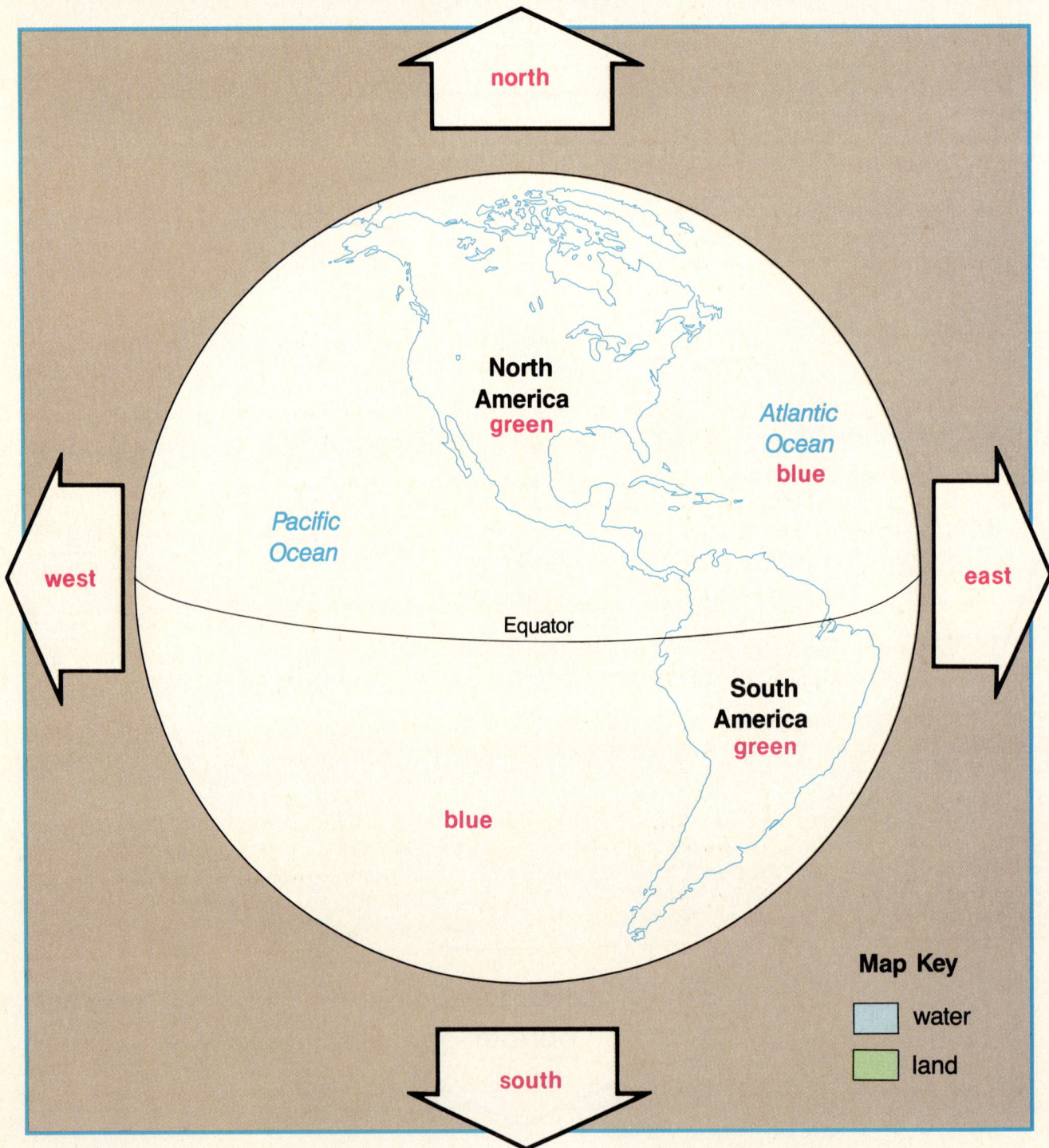

1. Write north, south, east, and west in the arrows.
2. Color the water blue.
3. Color the land green.

Name _____

Finding Places on a Globe

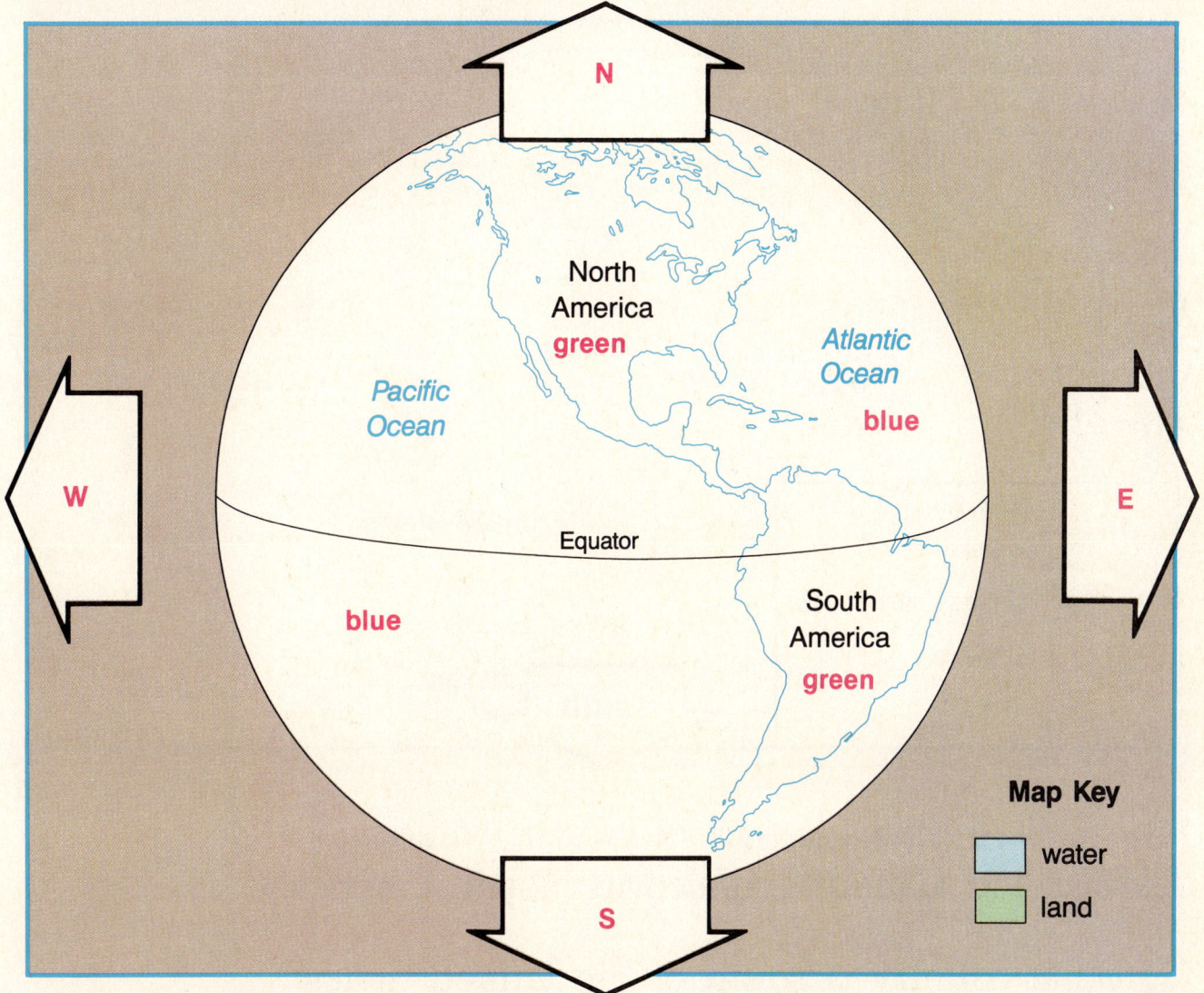

1. Write <u>N</u>, <u>S</u>, <u>E</u>, and <u>W</u> in the arrows.
2. Color the globe to match the map key. **Colors similar to the map key**
3. Look at the land on the map.
4. Find the water to the east of the land.
5. It is called the Atlantic _____**Ocean**_____.

PRACTICE 43

Finding Places on a Globe

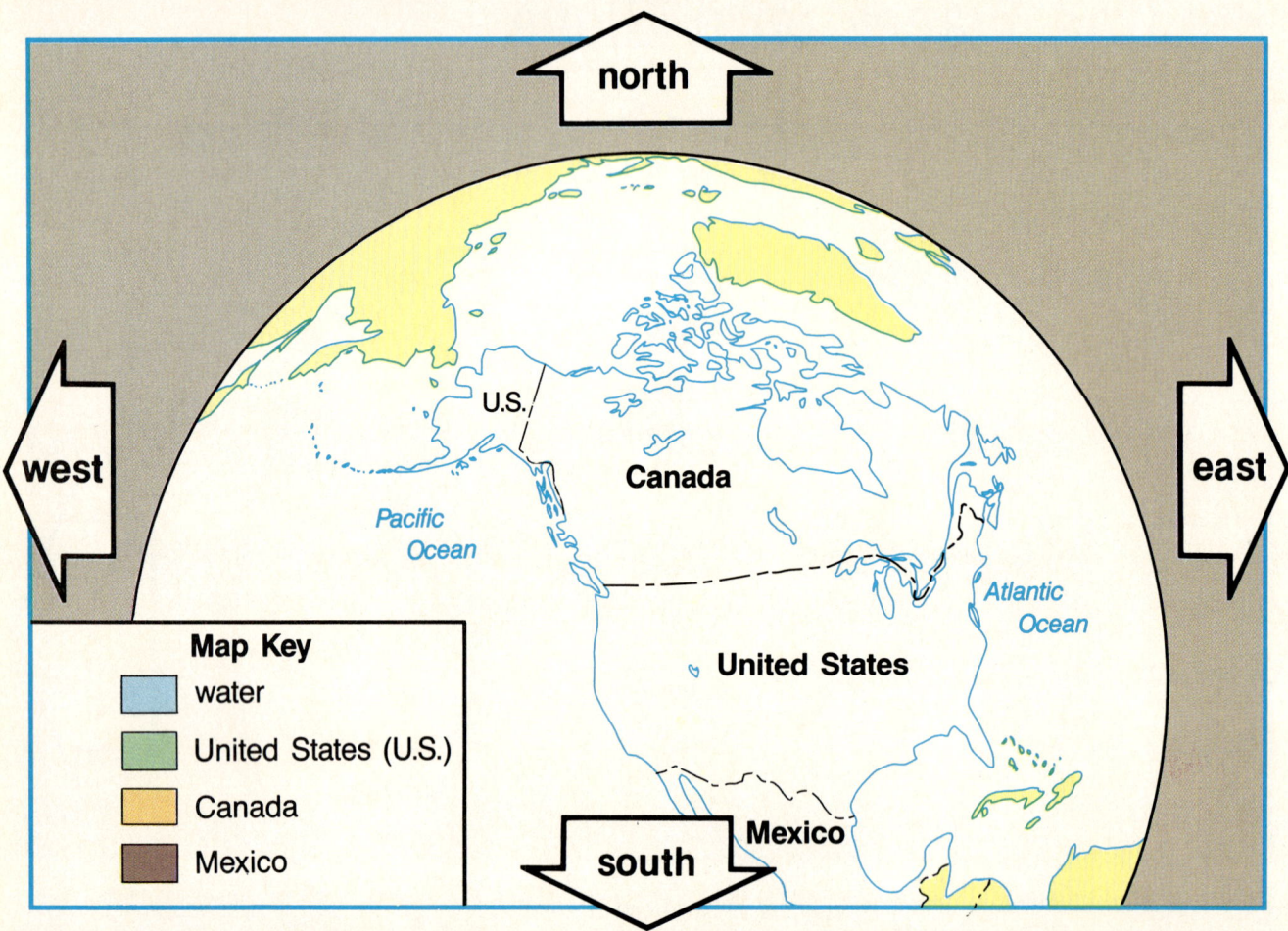

The United States is part of North America. Mexico and Canada are also in North America.

1. What country is south of the United States?

   Mexico

2. What country is north of the United States?

   Canada

3. Color the map to match the map key. **Colors similar to the map key**

Name _____

Skill Check

Words I Know   **globe   model**

A _____globe_____ looks like the earth.

Reading a Globe

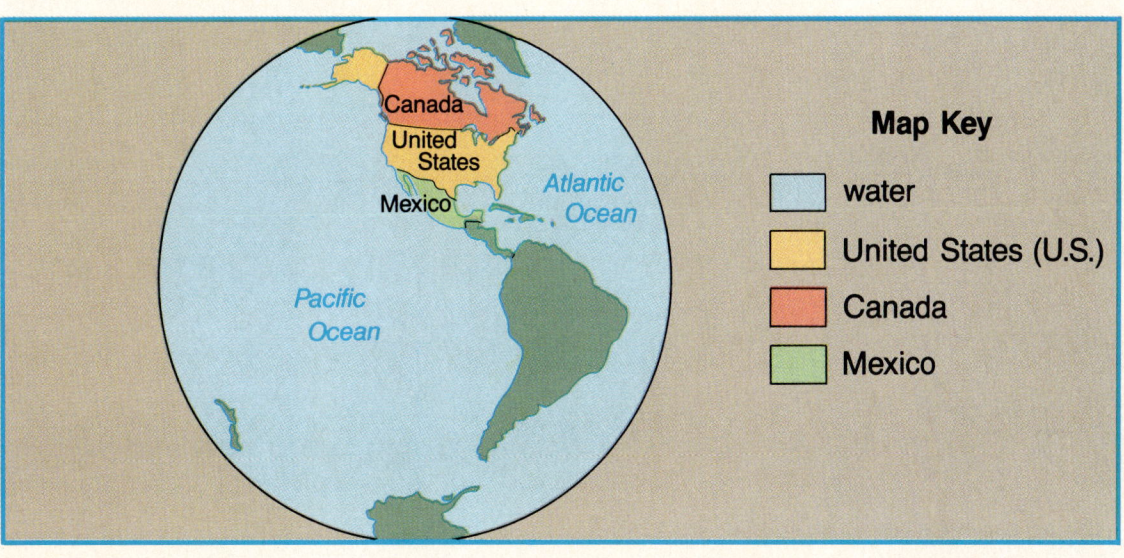

1. The Atlantic Ocean is _____east_____ of the United States.

2. Canada is _____north_____ of the United States.

3. Mexico is _____south_____ of the United States.

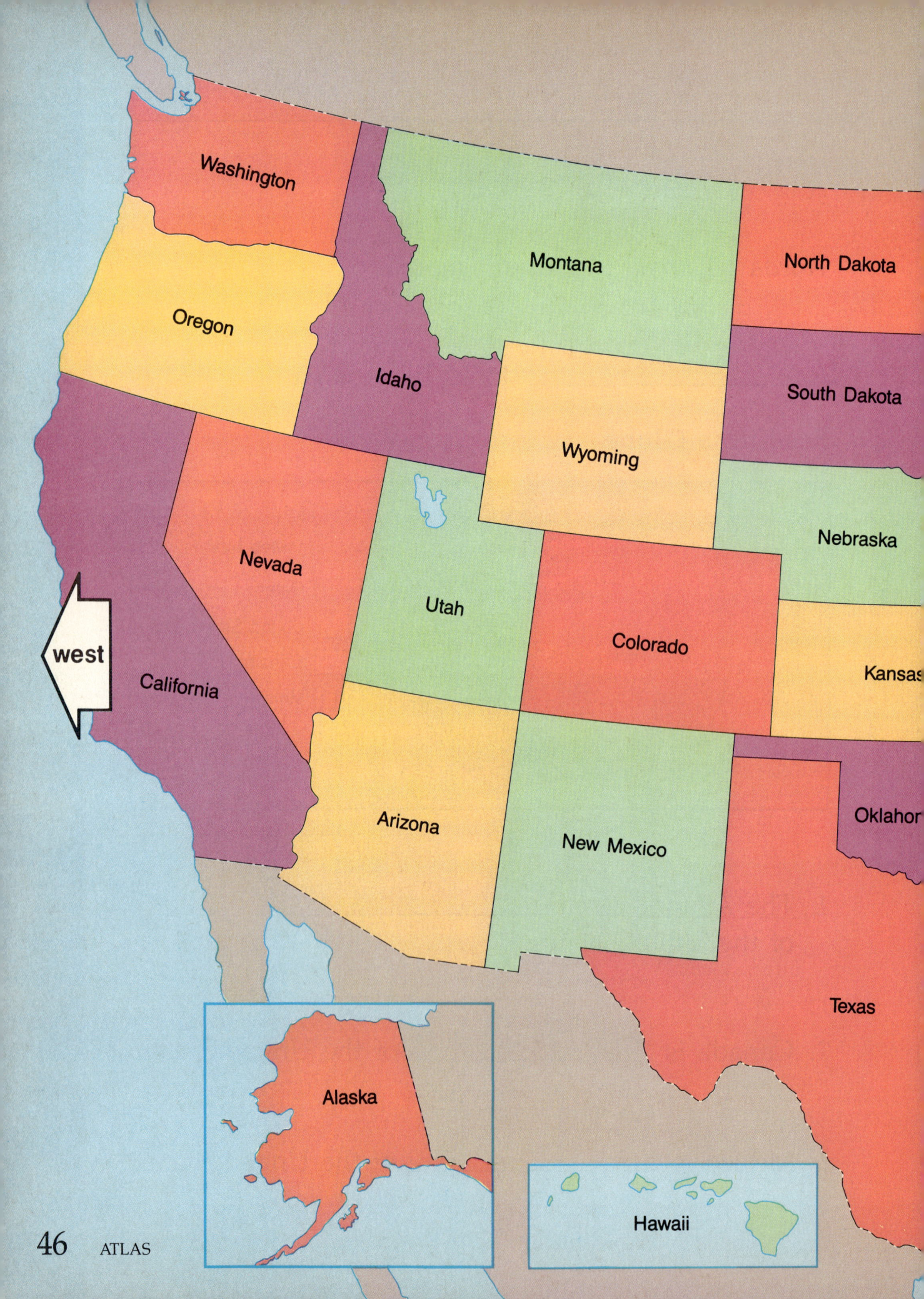

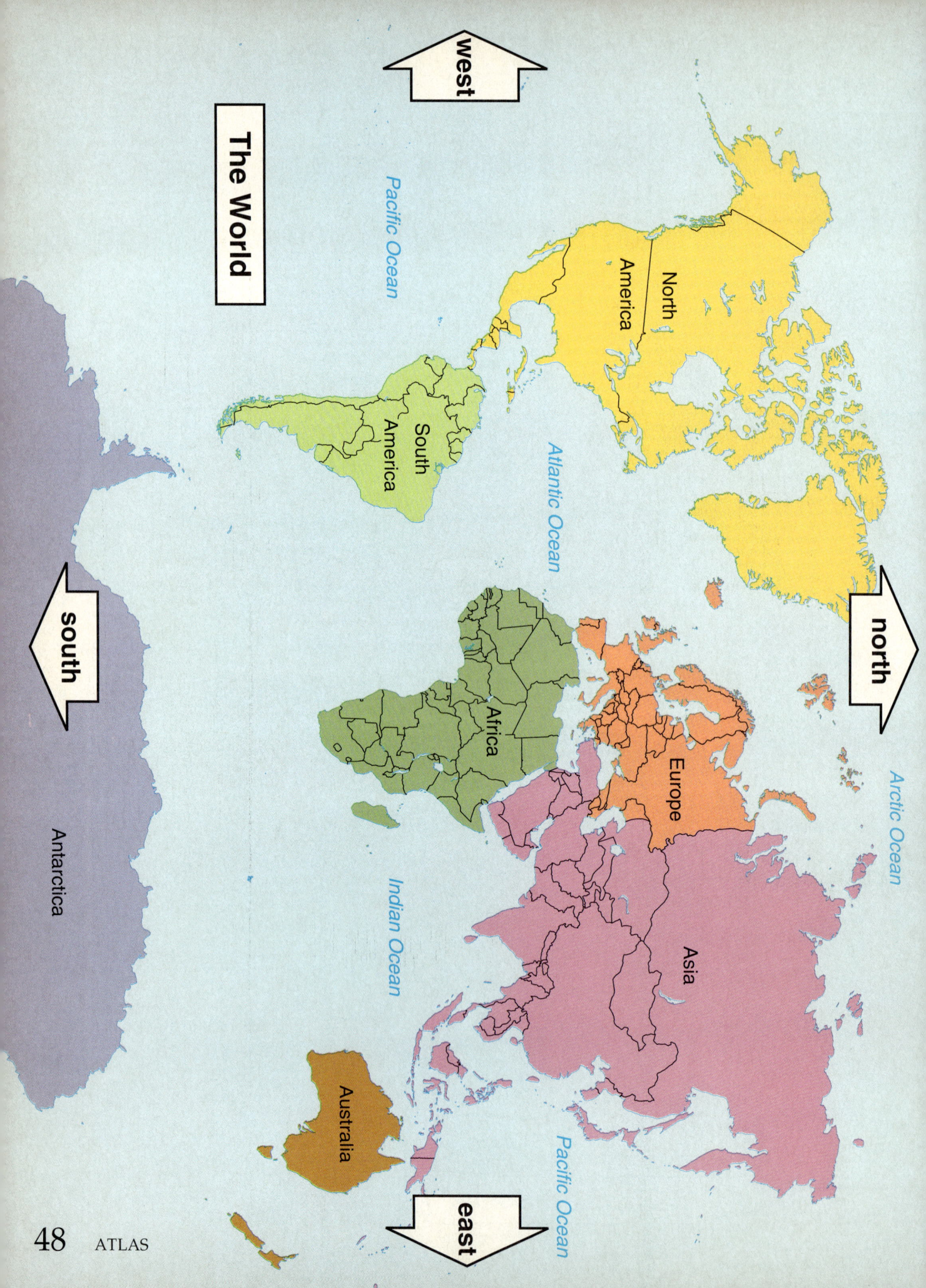

7 · Globes

STUDENT PAGES 40–45

OBJECTIVES

Students will
- use a map key to color a globe
- distinguish land and water on a globe
- locate the United States, Canada, and Mexico on a globe
- locate countries and oceans using directions

VOCABULARY

globe	Atlantic Ocean
model	Pacific Ocean
North America	United States (U.S.)
South America	Mexico
Equator	Canada

INTRODUCING THE SKILL

▶ Show students a globe. Demonstrate how places, such as the United States, can be found on the globe. Discuss the colors used on the globe to show land and water. Identify the Atlantic Ocean, Pacific Ocean, North Pole, South Pole, and Equator.

▶ Divide the class into groups. Distribute copies of the blackline on page T14 to students. Have them use the cut-out car, boat, and plane to take imaginary trips between places on a globe. Ask students to name the direction they are traveling. Provide students with copies of the blackline map of the world on page T18 to trace their route.

▶ Have students blow up large balloons and cover them with papier-mâché. After the papier-mâché has dried, have students paint the oceans and continents to make a globe. Hang the globes from the ceiling.

TEACHING NOTES

Page 40 Show students a globe with continents, countries, etc., labeled on it and have them compare and contrast the globe with the photo of the earth on page 40. First ask how they are the same. (They both show that the earth is round and made up of water and land.) Then ask how they are different. (The globe uses labels and is shown in colors that are different from the real earth.) To give students an easy way to visualize their location on the earth, draw a small person on heavy paper with tabs below the feet. Cut the person out and fold one tab forward and one tab back so that your person can stand up on a globe. Tape the person above your location on the globe.

Page 41 Explain to students that they live on the continent of North America. Show them North America on a globe and then have them circle it on the map on page 41. Tell students that the map shows only two continents, North America and South America, but that there are five other continents. Point out the other five continents on the globe. Slowly spin the globe and ask students if they think the earth is mostly land or water. When students answer "water," ask them what those large bodies of water are called (oceans). Show students the Atlantic Ocean and the Pacific Ocean on the globe, and have them draw a line under those two labels on the map.

Page 42 Show students the Equator on a globe and have them locate it on the map on page 42. Have them circle the label. Explain that the Equator is an imaginary circle that divides the earth in half. Next, show students the North Pole and the South Pole on the globe. Explain that the poles are the very top and bottom places on the earth. To demonstrate these concepts, use an orange or grapefruit. Show students the stem and tell them this represents the North Pole. Turn the fruit over and show them the bottom, which represents the South Pole. Now draw a line around the center to show the Equator. Cut the fruit in half to show that the Equator divides the earth in half.

EXTENSION ACTIVITIES

▶ Show students where Alaska and Hawaii are in relation to the rest of the United States. Have volunteers use a map or globe to locate the following: Canada, Mexico, the United States, their own home state, the Atlantic Ocean, and the Pacific Ocean.

▶ Give students copies of the globe blackline on page T15. First make one as a model. Then have each student color and cut out the globe. Help students glue it together at the North and South poles. Tape tab A to side B to form a sphere. Add tape at the poles to make it sturdier. Help students find the continents, oceans, and their own location on their globe.

AT HOME ACTIVITY

▶ Give students a copy of the blackline map of the world on page T18 to take home. Encourage students to ask family members to help them mark the map to show which countries their ancestors came from. Invite volunteers to share their maps with the rest of the class.

Name _____

Scarecrow and Symbols

T14   MAPS•GLOBES•GRAPHS   Level A   ©1993 Steck-Vaughn Company

Name _____

Globe

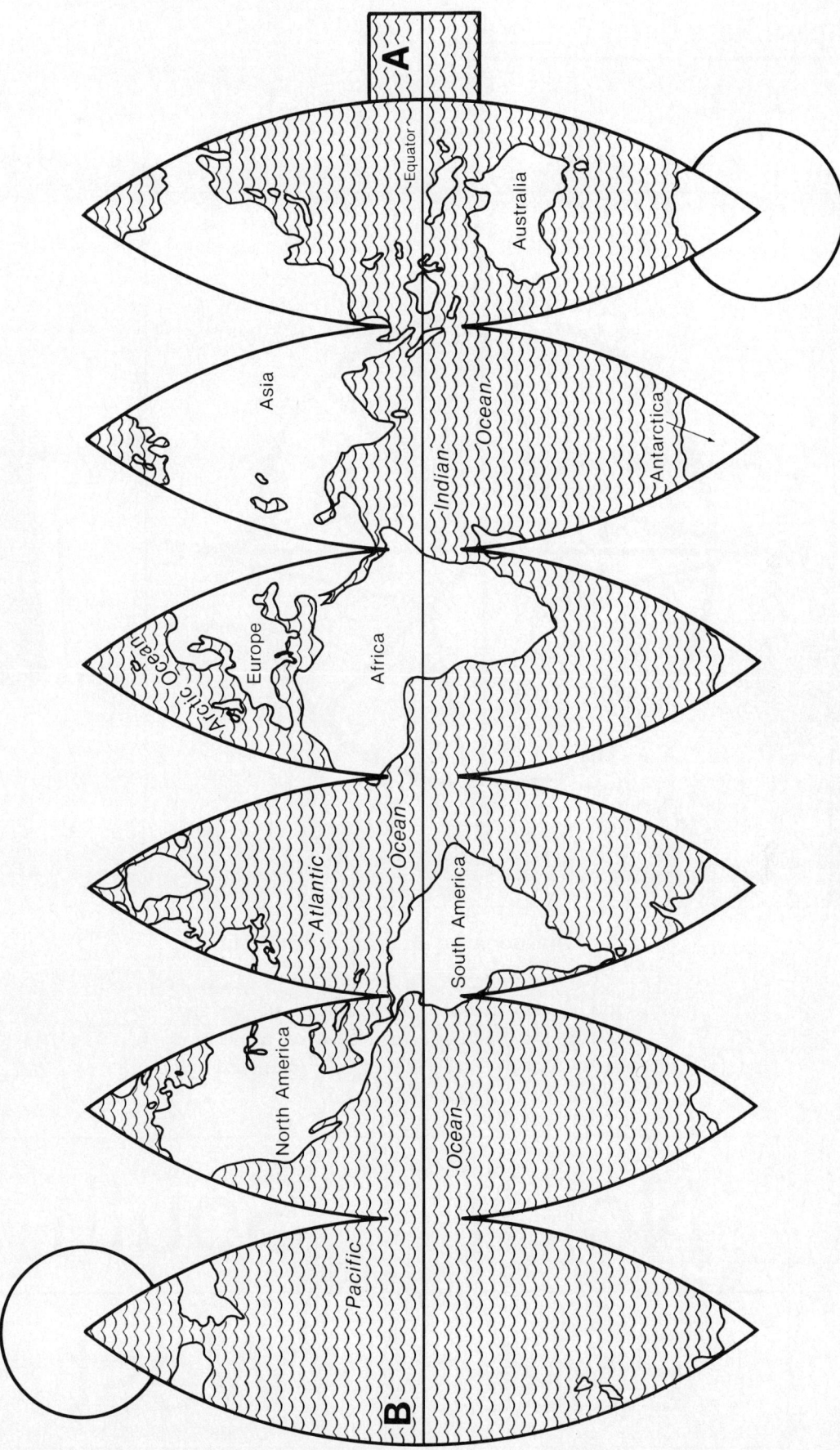

Name _____

Compass Rose Game Spinner

1 **2** **3** **4**
red green blue orange

Directions for Making Game Spinner

Color compass rose by number. Cut out and mount on a piece of cardboard. Cut out and mount the black spinner arrow on a piece of heavy paper. Attach the arrow to the compass rose with a brass fastener.

North	South
East	West

T16 MAPS•GLOBES•GRAPHS Level A ©1993 Steck-Vaughn Company

Name _____

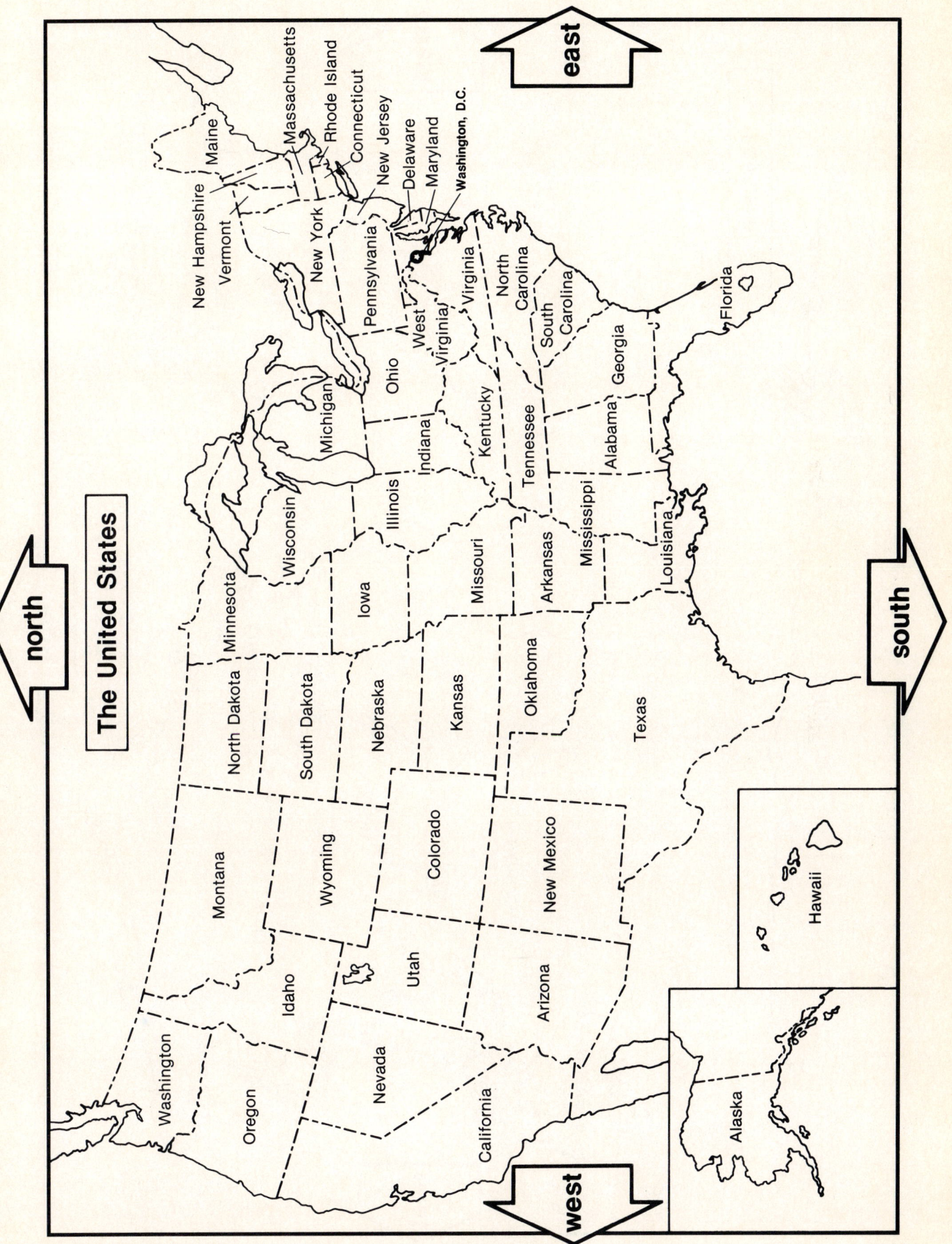

MAPS•GLOBES•GRAPHS   Level A   ©1993 Steck-Vaughn Company

Name _____

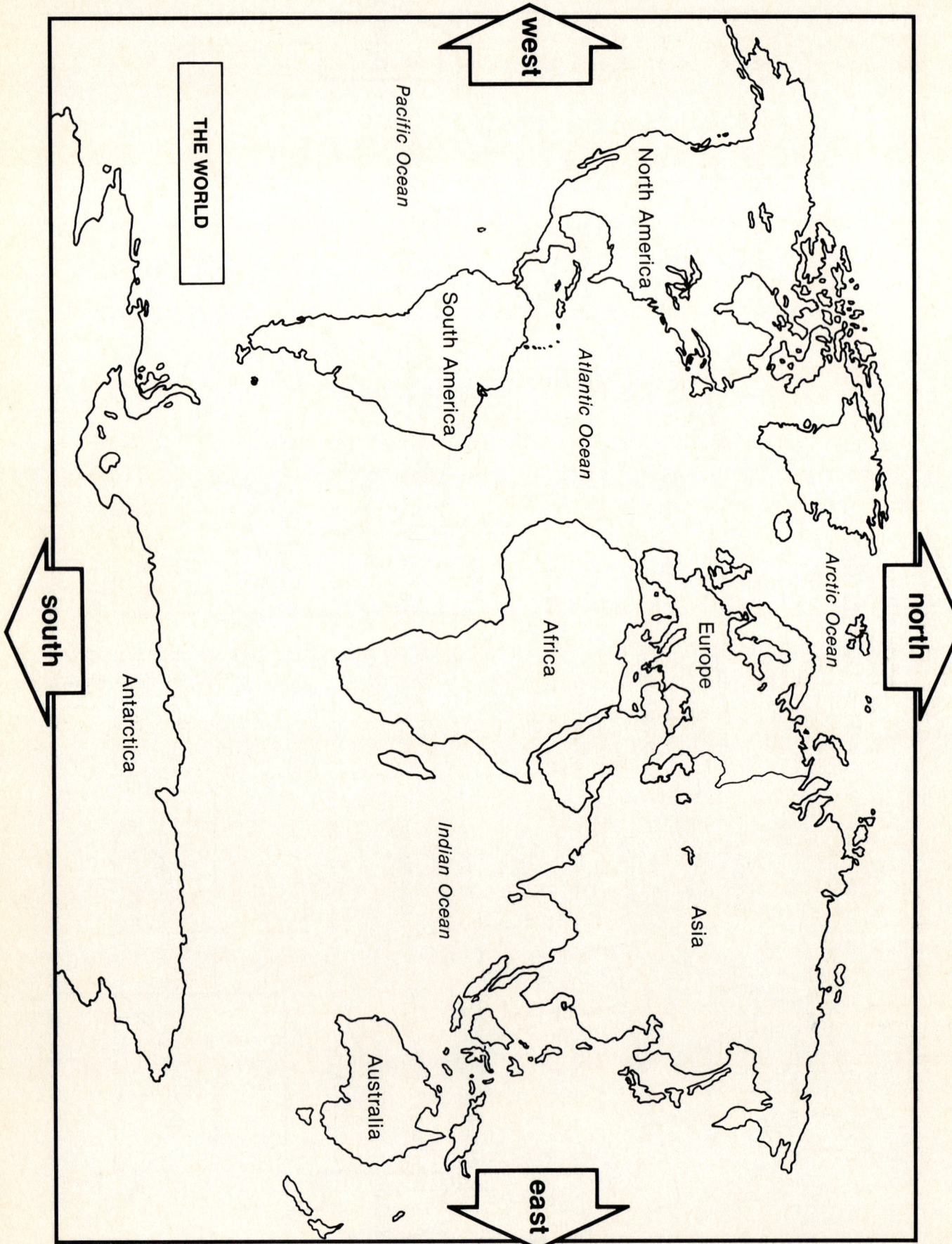

Name

Amusement Park Game Board

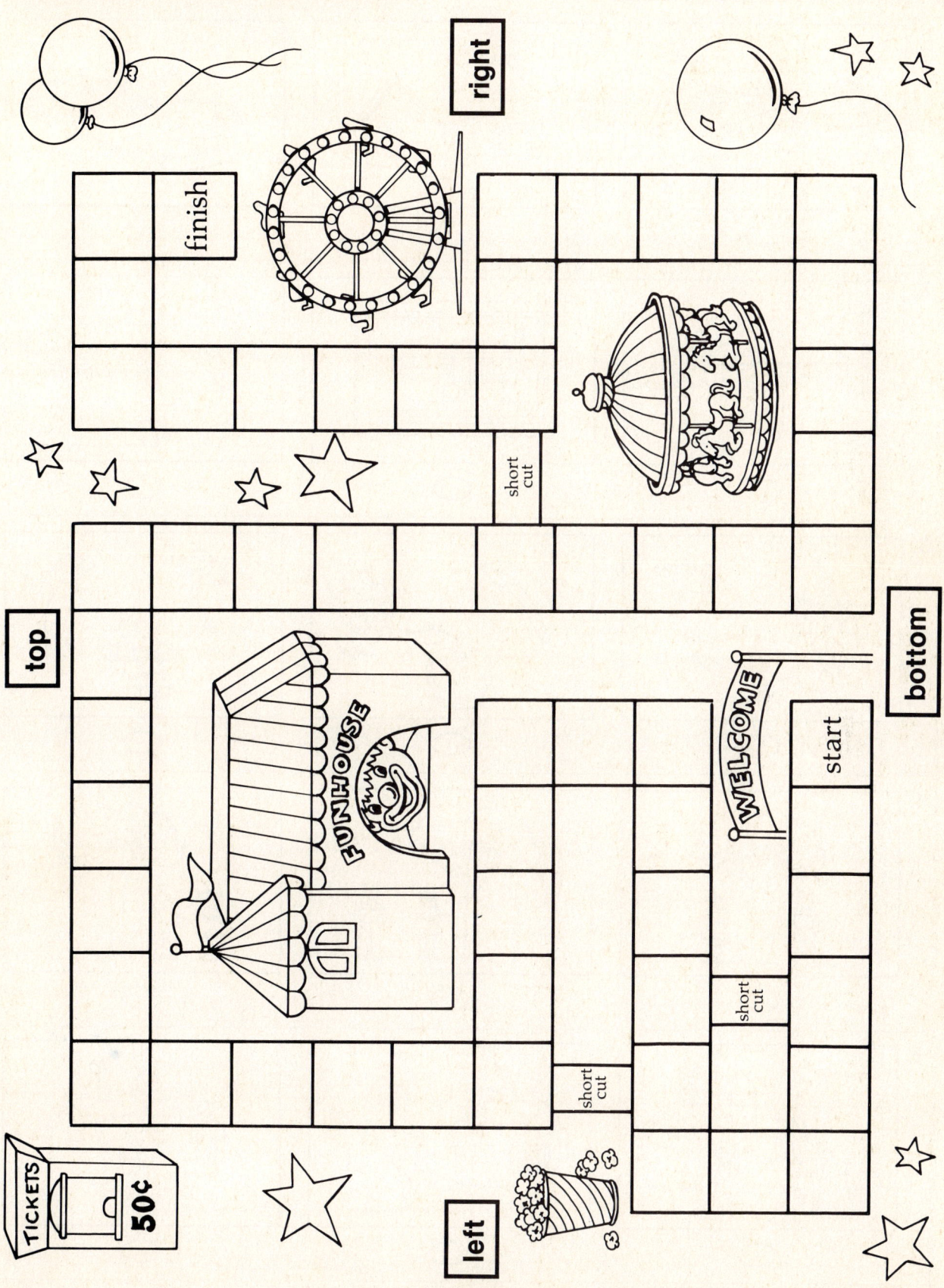

Name _____

Sample Standardized Test

T20 MAPS•GLOBES•GRAPHS Level A ©1993 Steck-Vaughn Company

Name

Sample Standardized Test

MAPS•GLOBES•GRAPHS Level A ©1993 Steck-Vaughn Company

T21

Sample Standardized Test Questions
To Be Read by Teacher to Students

Directions for Questions on Page T20

1. Look at the pictures in row 1. Which picture shows a drawing of a car? Mark the oval under the picture that shows a drawing of a car.
2. Look at the pictures in row 2. Which picture shows the way a school looks from above? Mark the oval under the picture that shows how a school looks from above.
3. Look at the pictures in row 3. Which picture shows the apple at the bottom? Mark the oval under the picture that shows the apple at the bottom.
4. Look at the pictures in row 4. Which picture shows the girl standing to the right of the boy? Mark the oval under the picture that shows the girl standing to the right of the boy.
5. Look at the pictures in row 5. Which picture shows the horse standing to the left of the barn? Mark the oval under the picture that shows the horse standing to the left of the barn.

Directions for Questions on Page T21

6. Look at the pictures in row 6. Which picture shows the teddy bear on the north side? Mark the oval under the picture that shows the teddy bear on the north side.
7. Look at the pictures in row 7. Which picture shows the elephant west of the lion? Mark the oval under the picture that shows the elephant west of the lion.
8. Look at the pictures in row 8. Which picture shows the car that is facing south? Mark the oval under the picture that shows the car that is facing south.
9. Look at the symbols in row 9. Which symbol stands for a house? Mark the oval under the symbol that stands for a house.
10. Look at the pictures in row 10. Which picture shows a globe? Mark the oval under the picture that shows a globe.

Answers appear below.

Page T20
1. ○ ○ ●   3. ○ ● ○   5. ● ○ ○
2. ○ ○ ●   4. ● ○ ○

Page T21
6. ○ ● ○   8. ○ ○ ●   10. ● ○ ○
7. ● ○ ○   9. ○ ● ○

Name _____

Glossary

bottom
page 22

Canada
page 44

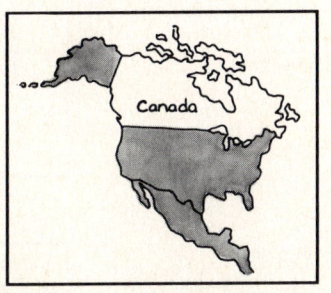

directions
page 28

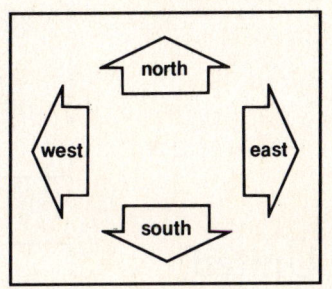

drawing
page 5

Earth
page 40

east
page 28

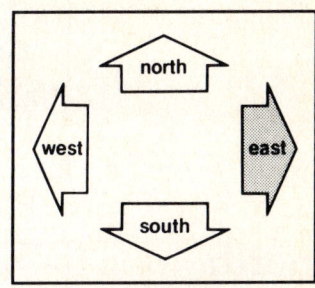

globe
page 40

left
page 22

map
page 17

map key
page 35

Mexico
page 44

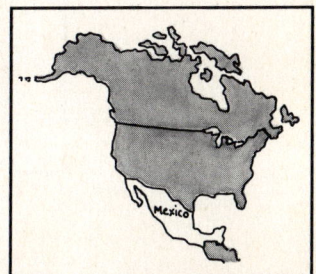

MAPS•GLOBES•GRAPHS   Level A   ©1993 Steck-Vaughn Company

Name _____

model
page 40

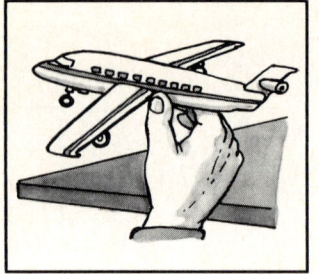

south
page 28

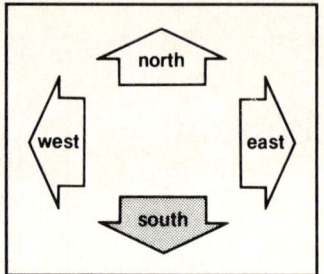

north
page 28

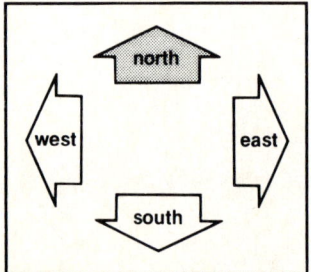

symbol
page 34

ocean
page 43

top
page 22

photo
page 4

United States
page 44

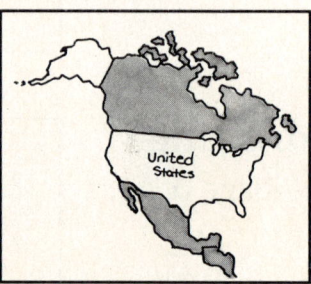

right
page 22

west
page 28

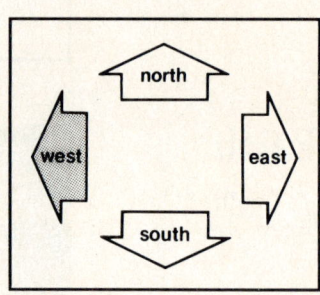